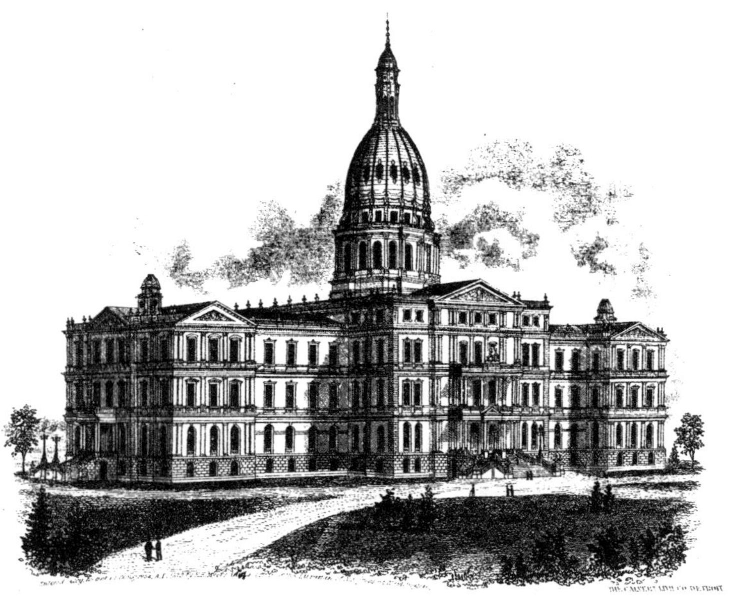

MICHIGAN STATE CAPITOL.

JOHN J. BAGLEY, Gov'r
E. O. GROSVENOR,
JAMES SHEARER,
ALEX. CHAPOTON,
} *Building Commissioners.*

E. E. MYERS, *Architect.*
N. OSBURN & Co., *Contractors.*
A. L. BOURS, *Secretary.*

Building commissioners

PROCEEDINGS

AT THE

Laying of the Corner Stone

GENERAL LIBRARY
University of
MICHIGAN

OF THE

New Capitol of Michigan,

On the 2d Day of October, 1873,

AT THE

CITY OF LANSING.

COMPILED BY
ALLEN L. BOURS,
Secretary of State Building Commissioners.

LANSING:
W. S. GEORGE & CO., PRINTERS AND BINDERS.
1873.

574
.12
.M6

Board of State Building Commissioners.

Governor JOHN J. BAGLEY, Chairman, . . . Detroit.

E. O. GROSVENOR, Vice President, . . . Jonesville.

JAMES SHEARER, ... Bay City.

ALEX. CHAPOTON, ... Detroit.

ALLEN L. BOURS, Secretary, ... Lansing.

ELIJAH E. MYERS, ... Architect.

OLIVER MARBLE, ... Local Superintendent.

N. OSBURN & Co., ... Contractors.

Officers of the Day.

PRESIDENT:

GOVERNOR JOHN J. BAGLEY.

VICE PRESIDENTS:

1 C. C. TROWBRIDGE, ... Detroit.
2 G. V. N. LOTHROP, ... Detroit.
3 E. J. PENNIMAN, ... Plymouth.
4 ALPHEUS FELCH, ... Ann Arbor.
5 WARNER WING, ... Monroe.
6 JOHN J. ADAM, ... Tecumseh.
7 G. T. GRIDLEY, ... Jackson.
8 C. P. DIBBLE, ... Battle Creek.
9 JOHN P. COOK, ... Hillsdale.
10 CHARLES UPSON, ... Coldwater.
11 J. G. WAIT, ... Sturgis.
12 R. W. LANDON, ... Niles.
13 JONATHAN J. WOODMAN, ... Paw Paw.
14 W. B. WILLIAMS, ... Allegan.
15 CHARLES E. STUART, ... Kalamazoo.
16 JOSEPH MUSGRAVE, ... Charlotte.
17 O. M. BARNES, ... Mason.
18 AMOS GOULD, ... Owosso.
19 J. B. WALKER, ... Flint.
20 A. C. BALDWIN, ... Pontiac.
21 R. P. ELDRIDGE, ... Mt. Clemens.
22 W. T. MITCHELL, ... Port Huron.
23 J. L. WOODS, ... Lexington.

24 ALBERT MILLER, ... Bay City.
25 D. H. JEROME, ... Saginaw.
26 JOHN LARKIN, ... Midland.
27 A. F. BELL, ... Ionia.
28 C. C. COMSTOCK, ... Grand Rapids.
29 W. M. FERRY, ... Grand Haven.
30 DELOS L. FILER, ... Manistee.
31 D. C. LEACH, ... Traverse Bay.
32 PETER WHITE, ... Marquette.

COMMITTEE OF ARRANGEMENTS:

GOV. JOHN J. BAGLEY,
E. O. GROSVENOR,
JAMES SHEARER,
ALEXANDER CHAPOTON,
DAVID ANDERSON,
AUGUSTUS S. GAYLORD,
JOHN HIBBARD,
JOHN P. HOYT,
LEONARD H. RANDALL,
ELLERY I. GARFIELD,
WILLIAM H. WITHINGTON,
OLIVER L. SPAULDING,
WILLIAM H. STONE,
JOHN S. TOOKER.

SECRETARY:

ALLEN L. BOURS, Lansing.

ASSISTANT SECRETARIES:

1 FRED. MORLEY, ... Detroit.
2 M. D. HAMILTON, ... Monroe.
3 JAMES O'DONNELL, ... Jackson.
4 JAMES H. STONE, ... Kalamazoo.
5 A. B. TURNER, ... Grand Rapids.
6 JOHN N. INGERSOLL, ... Corunna.
7 H. G. CHAPIN, ... Caro.
8 R. L. WARREN, ... East Saginaw
9 J. R. DEVEREAUX, ... Houghton.

Order of Proceedings.

The Corner-Stone of the new Capitol of the State of Michigan, was laid in the city of Lansing, on Thursday, the second day of October, 1873.

A procession was formed under the direction of General WILLIAM HUMPHREY, Chief Marshal, in accordance with the following orders:

Programme of Ceremonies.

The following will be the order of the formation of the column on the occasion of laying the Corner-Stone of the New State Capitol, at Lansing, October 2d, 1873:

The column will be in six divisions:

The First Division will form on Washington avenue, the LEFT resting on *Main street.*

The Second Division will form on St. Joseph street, west of, and with its RIGHT resting on, *Washington avenue.*

The Third Division will form on Hillsdale street, west of, and with its RIGHT resting on, *Washington avenue.*

The Fourth Division will form on Lenawee street, west of, and with its RIGHT resting on, *Washington avenue.*

The Fifth Division will form on Kalamazoo street, west of, and with its RIGHT resting on, *Washington avenue.*

The Civic Division will form on the plat in front of the old State Capitol.

Formation of Procession.

DETACHMENT OF POLICE,

In charge of Sergeant P. W. GIRARDIN.

CHIEF MARSHAL,

GEN. WM. HUMPHREY.

AIDS,

Col. F. SCHNEIDER, Capt. CHARLES HODSKIN, Capt. S. H. ROW, Capt. G. M. HASTY, E. H. BURT, Dr. GEO. E. RANNEY.

I.

MILITARY.

II.

CIVIC.

III.

COMMANDERIES OF KNIGHTS TEMPLAR.

IV.

MASONIC FRATERNITY.

V.

ENCAMPMENT I. O. OF O. F.

VI.

THE FRATERNITY OF I. O. OF O. F.

Arrangement of Divisions.

FIRST DIVISION.

MARSHAL,

GEN. W. H. WITHINGTON.

AIDS,

Major JOHN D. CLARK, Capt. ADAM BEATTIE, Lieut. BENJ. B. BERRY, WILLIAM H. MARSTON.

First U. S. Infantry Band.

Battalion First U. S. Infantry, Capt. R. H. OFFLEY, U. S. A., Commanding.

Co. —, First U. S. Infantry, Capt. G. S. GALLUPE, Commanding.

Co. —, First U. S. Infantry, Capt. E. WALKER, Commanding.

Battalion of State Troops, Capt. JAMES M. HINCKLEY, Commanding,

Detroit Light Guard, Capt. DAVID F. FOX, Commanding.

Porter Zouaves, Ann Arbor, Capt. WARREN E. WALKER, Commanding.

National Guard, Detroit, Capt. JOHN O'KEEFE, Commanding.

Adrian Light Guard, 1st Lieut. WHEELER, Commanding.

Tecumseh Zouaves, Capt. JAMES D. SHOLES, Commanding.

Monroe Light Guard, Capt. CHAS. F. GRUNER, Commanding.

Coldwater Light Guard, Capt. GEORGE H. TURNER, Commanding.

Hudson Light Guard, Capt. L. H. SALISBURY, Commanding.

Flint Union Blues, Capt. O. F. LOCKHEAD, Commanding.

Grand Rapids Guard, Capt. ISAAC C. SMITH, Commanding.

Ypsilanti Light Guard, Capt. CICERO NEWELL, Commanding.

Kalamazoo Light Guard, Capt. JOHN D. SUMNER, Commanding.

BATTALION OF CADETS.

Detroit Cadets; 2 Companies.

Monroe Cadets; 1 Company.

CIVIC DIVISION.

MARSHAL,

BRIG. GEN. JOHN ROBERTSON, Adj. General.

Constantine Band.

GOV. JOHN J. BAGLEY, President of the Day.

Governor's Staff.

WILLIAM A. HOWARD, Orator of the Day.

Right Rev. SAMUEL A. MCCOSKRY, D.D., LL.D.

Rev. NOAH FASSETT.

Invited Guests.

Capitol Commissioners and Architect.

Committee of Arrangements.

Maj. Gen. PHILIP ST. GEORGE COOKE, U. S. A., Commanding Department of the Lakes, and Staff.

Officers of United States Engineers, and other United States Military Officers.

Vice Presidents of the Day.

Secretary and Assistant Secretaries.

Senators and Representatives in Congress.

Judges of the United States Courts.

Judges of State Supreme and Circuit Courts.

Lieutenant Governor, Speaker of the House of Representatives.

Senators and Representatives of the State Legislature.

Lieut. Governor, Speaker of the House of Representatives.

Senators and Representatives of the Legislature of 1871.

State Officers.

Past State Officers.

President, Regents, and Professors of the State University.
Mayor and Common Council of the City of Lansing.
Mayors of other Cities, and Presidents of Villages.
Officers of United States Civil Departments.
Members of State Military Board.

SECOND DIVISION.

COMMANDERIES OF KNIGHTS TEMPLAR OF THE STATE OF MICHIGAN,

ELLERY I. GARFIELD,

Right Eminent Grand Commander, in command.

AIDS OF GRAND COMMANDER,

V. E. Sir L. H. RANDALL, D. G. C., Chief of Staff; Em. Sir S. C. RANDALL, G. C. G., Executive Officer; Em. Sir S. S. MATHEWS, Grand Gen.; Em. Sir Rev. A. J. DAVIS, Grand Prelate; Em. Sir R. J. CARNEY, G. S. Warden; Em. Sir C. E. GRISSON, G. J. Warden; Em. Sir M. S. SMITH, G. Treasurer; Em. Sir WM. P. INNES, G. Recorder; Em. Sir H. F. KNAPP, G. Stand. Bearer; Em. Sir MILLS H. LANDON, G. Sword B.; Em. Sir WM. B. WILSON, G. Warder; Em. Sir ALEX. MCGREGOR, G. Sentinel; and all Past Grand Officers.

The following Sir Knights have also been appointed on the Staff, and will be assigned to special duty: Col. Sir GEORGE LOCKLEY, Gen. Sir MARK FLANIGAN, Col. Sir WILLIAM PHELPS, Sir W. H. BURKE, Sir A. H. WEST, Sir D. P. SMILEY.

The Grand Commander and staff will be mounted.

The following Commanderies and the Commanders of each:

LANSING, 25, Lansing, . . . ALFRED BIXBY.
DETROIT, 1, Detroit, . . . JOHN P. FISKE.
EUREKA, 3, Hillsdale, . . . GEORGE C. MUNROE.
ADRIAN, 4, Adrian, . . . JOHN W. FINCH.

DeMolai, 5, Grand Rapids, .	. Leonard H. Randall.
Peninsula, 8, Kalamazoo, .	Frank Henderson.
Jackson, 9, Jackson, . . .	George W. Baker.
Ionia, 11, Ionia, . . .	J. H. Kidd.
Niles, 12, Niles, ...	Mills H. Landon.
Ann Arbor, 13, Ann Arbor, .	Stephen M. Webster.
Fenton, 14, Fenton, . . .	J. Buckbee.
St. Bernard, 16, East Saginaw,	Edwin Saunders.
Marshall, 17, Marshall, . .	John W. Fletcher.
Monroe, 19, Monroe, . . .	George R. Hurd.
Corunna, 21, Corunna, . .	Hugh McCurdy.
Pilgrim, 23, Big Rapids, . .	Charles P. Bigelow.
St. Johns, 24, St. Johns, . .	Oliver L. Spaulding.
Bay City, 26, Bay City, . .	C. F. Gibson.
Lexington, 27, Lexington, .	A. M. Clark.
Howell, 28, Howell, . . .	Sardis F. Hubbell.
Three Rivers, 29, Three Rivers,	D. D. Thorp.

THIRD DIVISION.

MARSHAL,

Capt. JAMES H. BAKER.

AIDS,

Col. A. Cottrell, Lansing; Col. M. W. Quackenbush, Owosso; Capt. H. B. Carpenter, Lansing; E. C. Chapin, Lansing; Capt. E. B. Gifford, Ionia; Capt. H. Troop, Owosso; Joseph B. Bampton, Detroit; E. M. Marston, Lansing; E. V. Sanford, Lansing; Geo. M. Huntington, Mason.

The formation of this Division will be in the following order:

DETROIT LIGHT GUARD BAND.

First—Grand Lodge of F. & A. M. of the State of Michigan, in the following order:

Band.

Grand Sword Bearer, with drawn sword.
Grand Standard Bearer.
Grand Master, supported by two Grand Deacons with black rods.
Grand Pursuivant.

Grand Marshal.

A Past Master carrying the Book of Constitutions.
Deputy Grand Master, carrying the golden vessel with corn.
Senior Grand Warden, carrying the silver vessel with wine.
Junior Grand Warden, carrying the silver vessel with oil.
The Five Orders of Architecture.

Past Grand Masters.
Past Deputy Grand Masters.
Past Grand Wardens.
Bible, Square and Compass, carried by a Master of a Lodge, supported by two Stewards with white rods.
Grand Chaplain.
Grand Treasurer, Grand Secretary, and Grand Lecturer.
District Deputy Grand Masters.
Grand Architect and Ass'ts, with Square, Level, and Plumb.
Grand Stewards, with white rods.
Grand Tiler, with drawn sword.

Second—Masonic Lodges in the following order:

UNION of S. O., No. 3, Detroit, .	R. S. DILLON, W. M.
EVERGREEN, No. 9, St. Clair, .	D. D. ODELL, W. M.
MURAT, No. 14, Albion, . .	E. P. ROBERTSON, W. M.
UNION, No. 28, Union City, .	E. MCDONALD, W. M.
FIDELITY, No. 32, Hillsdale, . .	S. S. SMITH, W. M.
LANSING, No. 33, Lansing, .	GEO. H. GREEN, W. M.
LYONS, No. 37, Lyons, . . .	D. C. SPAULDING, W. M.
PLYMOUTH ROCK, No. 47, Plymouth,	W. E. SMITH, W. M.
CLIMAX, No. 59, West Leroy, .	N. J. KELSEY, W. M.
LEXINGTON, No. 61, Lexington, .	A. M. CLARK, W. M.
EATON RAPIDS, No. 63, Eaton Rapids,	J.S. MONTGOMERY, W. M.
MASON, No. 70, Mason, . .	D. CAMPBELL, W. M.
GERMANIA, No. 79, Saginaw City,	A. W. ACHARD, W. M.

BYRON, No. 80, Byron, . .	A. MCCAUGHNA, W. M.
LOWELL, No. 90, Lowell, . .	A. J. HOWK, W. M.
GREENVILLE, No. 96, Greenville,	WM. MAXTED, W. M.
ST. JOHNS, No. 105, St. Johns, .	A. J. WIGGINS, W. M.
BAY CITY, No. 129, Bay City, .	WM. R. TUPPER, W. M.
STOCKBRIDGE, No. 130, Stockbridge,	C. W. VAN SLYKE, W. M.
MYSTIC, No. 141, Bronson Prairie,	EDWARD A. GAY, W. M.
SAGINAW VALLEY, No. 154, Saginaw,	W. W. KNIGHT, W. M.
DANSVILLE, No. 160, Dansville, .	M. M. ATWOOD, W. M.
GRAND LEDGE, No. 179, Grand Ledge,	J. W. MCMILLAN, W. M.
CHESANING, No. 194, Chesaning, .	J. L. HELME, W. M.
BEDFORD, No. 207, Bedford, .	C. W. ELDRED, W. M.
OKEMOS, No. 252, Okemos, . .	J. F. SMILEY, W. M.
DEWITT, No. 272, DeWitt, .	M. F. WHITE, W. M.
SPRINGPORT, No. 284, Springport,	F. H. LUDLOW, W. M.
SALT RIVER, No. 288, Salt River, .	RICHARD HOY, W. M.
WOODLAND, No. 304, Woodland, .	J. P. PHILLIPS, W. M.
ST. CHARLES, U. D., . . .	St. Charles.

FOURTH DIVISION.

MARSHAL,

CAPT. J. A. ELDER.

AIDS,

EUGENE B. WOOD, Lansing; WILLIAM APPLETON, Lansing; JOHN W. EDMONDS, Lansing.

Formation will be in the following order:

Lansing Cornet Band.
Wildey Encampment No. 4, I. O. O. F., Jackson.
Washington Encampment No. 19, I. O. O. F., Saginaw.
Valley Encampment No. 20, I. O. O. F., East Saginaw.
Friendship Encampment No. 33, I. O. O. F., Lansing.
Kanonda Encampment No. 36, I. O. O. F., Bay City.
And other Encampments in the order of rank.

FIFTH DIVISION.

MARSHAL,

JOHN N. INGERSOLL.

AIDS,

B. PRELL of Detroit; O. W. OVIATT of St. Joseph.

Lodges of Odd Fellows in the order of rank.

THE divisions will form on the streets indicated, at 12 o'clock M. The signal for the formation of the divisions will be the firing of one gun.

Marshals will be as prompt as possible in the formation of their divisions.

The movement of the column will commence at the firing of the second gun. As that portion of the column on Washington avenue uncovers the streets on which the several divisions are formed, the divisions will move into their proper places in the column.

The line of march will be down Washington avenue, passing in review before the Governor and staff, in front of the old Capitol, to Ottawa street, west on Ottawa street to Capitol avenue, north on Capitol avenue. From Capitol avenue to Washington avenue, south on Washington avenue to Ottawa street, east on Ottawa street to Grand street, south on Grand street to Allegan street, from which point the first division will move west on Allegan street to Washington avenue, north on Washington avenue to Michigan avenue, west on Michigan avenue to the new Capitol Grounds. The remainder of the column will continue south from Allegan street on Grand street to Washtenaw street, west on Washtenaw street, thence to its place in the column in the rear of the Civic Division, which will have taken its place immediately in the rear of the First Division.

Arriving at the Capitol Grounds, the First Division will be formed in the position indicated in column, by companies closed in mass.

The Civic Division will be conducted to the platform about the speakers' stand.

The Third Division will be formed on the left of the First Division, in column by commanders, closed in mass.

The Fourth Division will move to its position, immediately east of the foundation walls of the Capitol, and will be formed in close column.

The Fifth Division will be formed at the left of the Fourth Division, in close column.

The badge of the Chief Marshal and his aids will be yellow; of the Marshal and aids of the Military Division, red; the Knights Templar will appear in the uniform of their order; the badges of the Marshal and aids of the Masonic Fraternity, blue; the Encampments of I. O. O. F. will appear in the uniform of their order; the color of the badges of the Marshal and aids of Division of Lodges of I. O. O. F. will be purple.

Marshals of Divisions will have entire control of the formation of their respective Divisions, and of the changes of formation during the time of moving.

The procession will not re-form after the completion of the ceremony of laying the Corner-Stone. The military companies and Commanderies of Knights Templar will move from the ground, in charge of their respective company and Commandery commanders.

Detail instructions will be given by the Chief Marshal during the day.

WILLIAM HUMPHREY,
Chief Marshal.

Ceremonies at the Laying of the Corner-Stone.

MUSIC BY CROSETTE'S CORNET BAND.

INTRODUCTORY ADDRESS.

BY GOVERNOR JOHN J. BAGLEY.

FELLOW-CITIZENS—In the name of the constituted authorities of the State, I bid you welcome to its capital. We have assembled for the purpose of laying the corner-stone of a new Capitol building, worthy of our State; a fitting home for the different branches of its government. To those of us who have watched the growth of Michigan from infancy to manhood, the occasion recalls the toils and trials of early days, the anxieties and cares of pioneer life; while a pardonable egotism, as we look about us, tells of battles fought and victories won over Nature in her most rugged mood. To-day we stand here as conquerors of forest and swamp, and can proudly say: "If thou seekest a beautiful peninsula, behold it here."

In olden time temples and public buildings were erected, not alone for use, but as memorials of king or conqueror, and inscribed with records of their valor and heroism. The temples have crumbled into dust—king and conqueror are forgotten—metal and granite have disappeared—time has conquered all. And so it will be. But our greater civilization, with its triumphs and inventive art and skill, makes it certain that, though buildings may crumble away and nations vanish, there will yet be left, somewhere, the history of to-day and all future days. Our record will be preserved. We shall not be judged in the distant future by the ruins of our buildings, dug up by the antiquary, but by the record of our deeds as individuals and communities, by our public acts, by our legislation, by our care for the public good. If we make moral worth, honesty of purpose, and integrity of soul the pathway to public position—if our legislation is kept pure and sweet—if the common good is the common law, we shall leave behind us a history more enduring than brick or marble, a heritage richer than gold or precious stones. May this be the ambition of our time, and our hope for the future; remembering, always, that

> "The riches of the commonwealth,
> Are free, strong minds, and hearts of health;
> And more to her than gold or grain,
> The cunning hand and cultured brain."

PRAYER.

BY RIGHT REV. SAMUEL A. McCOSKRY, D. D., LL. D.

ALMIGHTY AND MERCIFUL GOD! We come before Thee, as children to a father. Thou hast created us, and redeemed us. Thou has brought us into the closest relationship with Thyself, unworthy as we are, and undeserving of Thy kindness and care. Thy mercies are new every morning, and repeated every evening. We come before Thee with confidence, for Thou hast invited us to come,—with deep humility, for Thou art holy, and we are prone to sin against Thee,—with hope, for Thou hast promised to pardon and bless us. May our hearts be warmed with love to Thee for Thy unnumbered mercies to us. May we fear to offend Thee, and enable us to make Thy law the rule and guide of our life. Enable us, by Thy grace, to give our hearts and lives to Thee, the only return which Thou requirest for all the blessings we have received. We thank Thee for the goodly heritage which Thou hast given us; for the civil and religious privileges which we enjoy, and for the multiplied manifestations of Thy favor towards us. We thank Thee that Thou didst give wisdom to the fathers of our country, to lay the foundations of peace, liberty, and safety. We bless and adore Thy glorious Majesty for this Thy loving kindness and providence, and we humbly pray that the devout sense of this signal mercy may renew and increase in us a true spirit of love and thankfulness to Thee,—a spirit of obedience to Thy will,—a spirit of peaceable submission to the laws and government of our country,—a spirit of fervent zeal for our holy religion, which

Thou hast preserved to us, and which forms the basis of all our domestic, social, and civil happiness. Preserve, we beseech Thee, to our country the blessings of peace, and secure them to all the people of the earth. Bless Thy servant, the President of the United States, the Governor of this State, and all others in authority, and so rule their hearts and strengthen their hands, that they may punish wickedness and vice, and maintain Thy true religion and virtue. Look with favor, we beseech Thee, upon the services of this day. May the Corner-Stone, now to be laid in Thy fear, remind us of Thy watchful care over us, call forth continued thankfulness for Thy mercies, and excite us to a grateful and ready obedience to Thy will. May no unholy strife and contentions be found within these walls,—may truth and justice be always found therein, and may they long stand as a fitting monument of grateful and happy people, whose God is the Lord. Protect and guard all who are engaged in this work, from accident and danger. And finally, Merciful Father, when all the material temples of earth shall crumble and decay, may we be found fitted to dwell forever in that temple not made with hands, eternal in the heavens. All which we humbly ask, for the sake of our blessed Lord and Saviour. AMEN.

NATIONAL HYMN.

Tune—"AMERICA."

My country, 'tis of thee,
Sweet land of liberty,—
Of thee I sing:
Land where my fathers died,—
Land of the pilgrims' pride,—
From every mountain's side
Let freedom ring.

My native country, thee,
Land of the noble free,
Thy name I love:
I love thy rocks and rills,
Thy woods and templed hills,—
My heart with rapture thrills,
Like that above.

Our Father, God, to Thee,
Author of Liberty,—
To Thee we sing:
Long may our land be bright
With Freedom's holy light;
Protect us by Thy might,
Great God our King.

ORATION

BY

Hon. William A. Howard.

Your Excellency, Members of the Legislature, Ladies and Gentlemen—Citizens of Michigan:

What is the lesson of the passing hour? What means this pageant? Whence this multitude? Who are they? What brings them here? Why these upturned faces? Why this eagerness to catch every word? Why this all-absorbing interest in these ceremonies?

We are indeed citizens of a great commonwealth. Here is to arise a structure of vast proportions and beautiful designs, at great expense, and all to be paid for from the earnings of the people. It might have cost twice as much, and exceeded in architectural beauty the finest model of modern or ancient times, and yet excited little of the interest shown here to-day. We are not attracted by the magnificence of the proposed structure, nor do we come to pay homage to any architectural design, however beautiful. Why then this absorbing interest? It is because the structure here to arise is associated in our minds with that government "of the people, by the people, and for the people," which we call our public. It is because this edifice is to be dedicated to the enactment and administration of such equal laws as will tend "to establish justice, and to secure the blessings of liberty to ourselves and our posterity" for all time. That liberty, regulated by, and under the reign of, just and equal laws, laws that restrain the mere license of all, and thus secure the freedom of each to move in his or her own path of duty and of pleasure. As the planets, each in its own proper orbit, instead of flying athwart the heavens in every direction, producing confusion and chaos, contributes to steady all the rest; so every citizen of a well regulated State, by enjoying his own liberty, under the wholesome restraint of equal and just laws, aids in securing to others the like precious boon.

Our interest then centers, not in the magnificence of structure or beauty of design, but in the uses to which it is to be devoted. In short, we here erect the house of a great and free State. This raises the question, what is a State? When is a State truly great? When really free? Is Michigan such a State in its present condition or future prospects? It may be said a State cannot exist without a given amount of territory, with metes and bounds fixed with greater or less certainty. But the land or territory is far from being the State. We have found our 56,000 square miles of land, with fixed boundaries, a very good place in which to erect a State; but the land, with all its productive power, with its waving forests and mineral wealth, is far from being the State. With this territory, as a place to put a State, we are more than satisfied. The State of Michigan is not two score years old,--its territory was before Christopher Columbus.

For many years this peninsula remained *terra incognita;* in the apprehension of many, a myth—a horrid place, abounding in swamps and marshes, and the very home of diseases dire, uninhabited and uninhabitable. To penetrate it, you must take a canoe, and work your way through lagoons, soon to be stopped by disease, perchance death. To collect and rehearse the fabulous stories told, and sometimes believed, might, at this day, afford amusement, but after all would be a thriftless employment. Passing over the common gossip and fabulous canards of those early times, I content myself by citing such official action on the part of the government, as was believed to establish the worthlessness of what was then known as Michigan. On the 6th of May, 1812, Congress passed an act requiring that 2,000,000 acres of land should be surveyed in the then Territory of Louisiana, and a like quantity in the Territory of Illinois, north of the Illinois river, and the same quantity in the Territory of Michigan, in all 6,000,000 acres, to be set apart for the soldiers in the war with Great Britain. Each soldier was to have 160 acres of land fit for cultivation. The lands were surveyed and appropriated under this law in Louisiana and Illinois, but the surveyors reported that there were no lands in Michigan fit for cultivation. Accordingly, on the 29th of April, 1816, Congress passed an act repealing so much of the law of the 6th of May, 1812, as related to Michigan, and provided for taking 1,500,000 acres in Illinois, north of the Illinois river, and 500,000 acres in the Territory of Missouri, in lieu of the 2,000,000 acres which could not be found in Michigan. This would seem to be decisive. And yet, in 1830, fourteen years later, Michigan was found to have 31,698 inhabitants, of whom 3,688 lived in that portion of the then Territory, lying the west side of Lake Michigan; and in 1834, only eighteen years after the act of Congress referred to, this worthless territory was found to contain 87,273 inhabitants. Two years later they framed a State Constitution, adopted a great seal, and for a motto threw the broad challenge to the whole world, "*Si quæris Peninsulam amœnam circumspice.*"

In the Congressional legislation referred to, the Government showed its regard for its soldiers. It had too high an appreciation of the value of their services, to attempt to palm off on them the worthless lands of Michigan. Those Congressmen, in their simplicity, little thought that in less than fifty years, there would arise on this very territory, a great commonwealth, one of the sisterhood of States, that should send forth to the great war for the defense of the national life, more soldiers than the nation had ever mustered in any one of its wars; ninety thousand soldiers, who should not only "keep step to the music of the Union," but bear full high the national banner, and illustrate American valor on every battle-field, from the great lakes to the Gulf.

The legislation of Congress to which I have referred, was based on the report of the Surveyor General of Ohio, dated the 30th November, 1815, and on the 29th of April, 1816, was passed the repealing act, by which the soldiers were relieved of the supposed worthless lands of Michigan in payment of bounties. I need not weary you by reading here this report, but shall publish it in a note to the text of this address.* Much

---

* Extract from a letter of the Surveyor General of Ohio to the Commissioner of the General Land Office, dated Chillicothe, November 30, 1815, relative to the bounty land in Michigan, granted by act of May 6, 1812:

DEPUTY SURVEYOR'S REPORT.

"Description of the military lands in Michigan. The country on the Indian boundary line, from the mouth of the great Auglaize River, and running thence for about fifty miles, is (with some few exceptions) low, wet land, with a very thick growth of underbrush, intermixed with very bad marshes, but generally very heavily timbered with beech, cottonwood, oak, etc.; thence continuing north, and extending from the Indian

less can I rehearse the statistics, showing the progressive steps of development since that time. I should weary you and transcend the proper limits of this address, by even stating the aggregates of our varied industries; of the wealth developed already; of our inexhaustible mineral wealth and agricultural resources, our natural manufacturing facilities, the steady increase of our population, and the general prosperity of our people. Fortunately I am relieved from any such necessity. Under a wise provision of law, the Secretary of State is required to publish these statistics, carefully collected and collated; this duty has been carefully performed, and the volume is of easy access to all our people. Besides, the committee of arrangements have wisely provided for a brief

---

boundary eastward, the number and extent of the swamps increases, with the addition of numbers of lakes, from twenty chains to two and three miles across. Many of the lakes have extensive marshes adjoining their margins, sometimes thickly covered with a species of pine called 'tamarack,' and other places covered with a coarse, high grass, and uniformly covered from six inches to three feet (and more at times) with water. The margins of these lakes are not the only places where swamps are found, for they are interspersed throughout the whole country, and filled with water, as above stated, and varying in extent. The intermediate space between these swamps and lakes, which is probably near one-half of the country, is with a very few exceptions, a poor, barren, sandy land, on which scarcely any vegetation grows, except very small, scrubby oaks. In many places, that part which may be called dry land, is composed of little, short sand-hills, forming a kind of deep basins, the bottoms of many of which are composed of a marsh similar to the above described. The streams are generally narrow, and very deep compared with their width, the shores and bottoms of which are (with a very few exceptions) swampy beyond description; and it is with the utmost difficulty that a place can be found, over which horses can be conveyed.

"A circumstance peculiar to that country is exhibited in many of the marshes, by their being thinly covered with a sward of grass, by walking on which, evinced the existence of water or a very thin mud immediately under their covering, which sinks from six to eighteen inches from the pressure of the foot at every step, and at the same time rising before and behind the person passing over. The margins of many of the lakes and streams are in a similar situation, and in many places are literally afloat. On approaching the eastern part of the military lands, towards the private claims on the *Straights* and Lake, the country does not contain so many swamps and lakes, but the extreme sterility and barrenness of the soil continues the same. Taking the country altogether, so far as has been explored, and to all appearances, together with the information received concerning the balance, is so bad there would not be more than one acre out of one hundred, if there would be one out of one thousand, that would in any case admit of cultivation."

historic sketch of the most salient points of our progress, to be prepared by their secretary, and published with a report of this day's proceedings, which altogether supersedes the necessity of any elaborate statement in this connection.

I shall, therefore, content myself, under this branch of my subject, with placing in juxtaposition, statements drawn from the report, by which the worthlessness of Michigan was supposed to be officially established, and the facts as they actually exist under the present state of development. The report says: "Taking the country altogether, so far as has been explored, and to all appearances, together with information received concerning the balance, is so bad, there would not be more than one acre out of one hundred, if there would be one out of one thousand, that would in any case admit of cultivation."

Since the acquisition of the Upper Peninsula, in connection with the Toledo war, the whole area of Michigan, including both peninsulas, is about 35,000,000 acres, and, of course, one acre "out of one hundred" would be 350,000, and one acre "out of one thousand" would be 35,000 acres. Now, on the 1st of June, 1870, as appears by the census returns, we had over 5,000,000 acres under actual cultivation, and more than 10,000,000 of acres embraced in farms. These farms were of the cash value of $398,096,746.00, and their annual products were estimated at $82,171,561.00. The 10,000,000 of acres now embraced in farms, are but a portion of those that in "any case admit of cultivation," for already 20,000,000 of acres pay taxes as the property of individuals.

The report, after describing the country as consisting of near "one half swamps," and the other half a sterile, barren waste, says: "And it is with the utmost difficulty that a place can be found, over which horses can be conveyed." The only answer I can make to this, is to refer to the fact, that on the first of June, 1870, we had 229,274 horses, besides 2,362 mules and asses, and plenty of roads for them to travel on; and that the owners of some of these horses, think they can get around about as well as anybody's horses. It might be added in this connection, that in addition to finding places "over which horses can be conveyed," we have found places on which we have built more than three thousand miles of railroad.

The report proceeds: "*On approaching the eastern part of the military lands, toward the private claims on the Straights and Lake, the country does not contain so many swamps and lakes, but the extreme sterility and barrenness of the soil continues the same.*" The country here described must embrace parts of Lenawee, Washtenaw, Oakland, and the west part of Macomb, Wayne, and Monroe counties. I see many people here from that section of the State. I trust they will forgive me for citing that portion of the report. I may seem cruel. They, poor fellows, probably, were not aware that they lived in a country of "*extreme sterility and barrenness.*" In their blindness, they had supposed you would go far to find a country of equal extent of greater average productiveness, or a less proportion of waste land.

I have dwelt upon the statements of this report because of its official character, and of the controlling influence that the supposed correctness of its statements had upon important congressional legislation.

It shows that the framers of our first State constitution, by boldly challenging the world to look at this Peninsula, as in every way adapted to become the seat of a great and prosperous commonwealth, against popular prejudice and official action, exercised a boldness, courage, and self-reliance which do them great honor, while our present abundant and varied resources, developed and to be developed, show that Providence has placed here an exuberance of all those physical conditions necessary to the growth and maintenance of a great and prosperous State.

They did not claim to then have a State. They said, "*Si quæris Peninsulam amœnam circumspice.*" They pointed to this peninsula as eminently suited to be the place for a State.

We are told upon the highest authority, that "The powers that be, are ordained of God." And hence we may conclude, without presumption, that He who made the world and all things therein, He who formed this peninsula, with its productive power and its hidden treasures, wills that it should be not only the abode of his creatures, but the seat of a great, prosperous, and free State. All our physical development for the thirty-seven years; all our increase of wealth; all the unfolding of our vast natural resources, are but the adornment of the Peninsula, that she may the more effectively woo the Heavenly Pilgrim. As a bride adorns herself for her husband, so every successive day she puts on still more beautiful garments, and beckons the divinely appointed State to her bower. Her vast agricultural treasures, that block up the thoroughfares and crowd the marts of the world, all utter their voice,—all say "Come." Her hundreds of thousands of tons of iron ore that annually come forth from their mountain seat, and leap into all the channels of the commerce of the world, say "Come." Her rich and extensive copper mines say "Come." Her forests of boundless wealth wave their welcome, and say "Come." From year to year she displays her jewels, ever growing in brightness, and says with increased persuasiveness, "*Si quæris Peninsulam amœnam circumspice.*" The evidences are everywhere abundant that Providence designed and fitted this peninsula to be the abode of an industrious and happy people, the place of an advanced civilization, the seat of a great, prosperous, independent, and free State.

What, then, is a State, in distinction from the territory where it exists? A free government is simply the organized power of the good, consolidated and wielded to restrain the bad, and to protect the weak from the encroachments of the strong; or, in other words, to establish justice and secure the blessings of liberty to all the people. All courts interpret its will, and all executive officers execute its decrees. The sheriff goes forth with its processes, and even when supported by the *posse comitatus*, or the whole military power, he is only the minister of its will. Such a government is right in its conception and organization, andso far must receive the approbation of Heaven. "Order is Heaven's first law," and such a government, existing for, and securing the good of, the governed, is the "creature of God." We can hardly conceive of the existence of such a government, without admitting the truth of the fundamental axioms of the Declaration of Independence; for such a government can only rightfully exist by the consent of the governed, and for the good of the governed.

A *State* is the people in a given territory and their institutions.

A *Free State* consists of the people and such institutions as they make for themselves.

A *despotic State* consists of the people and such institutions as are imposed upon them.

A free State lives in the will of its people! Public sentiment shapes its course and controls its action! We judge of a State by the same rule as of an individual. "By their fruits ye shall know them." Their character must be determined by what they do; but if they do what public opinion demands, it is essential that public opinion should be enlightened and virtuous. Hence it has come to be an axiom, that the only true basis of a Republic is the intelligence and morality of its people. Experience goes far towards proving that the more closely the public morality is allied to, and springs from the personal religion of the individual citizens, the better it endures the trial. The basis of public morality is the enlightened consciences of individual citizens.

The first duty of every free State, commanded by the highest of all laws, the instinct of self preservation,—is to foster institutions for the promotion of the intelligence and virtue of its people. Michigan's first Governor, in his first message, warns us that the "liberty of a people cannot be forced beyond its intelligence." And he might have added, it cannot long survive the decay of public morality. Governments rise and fall, and nations decay and pass away, but the great principles that pertain to rightful government, remain unchanged and unchangeable. The Creator seems to have stamped his own immutability upon justice, and truth, and other like characteristics.

Another important function of a State, is to provide for the unfortunate,—the deaf and dumb, the blind, and the insane. Humanity requires this at the hands of the State, since a kind of treatment is often required, that friends and relatives could not furnish; nor could any system of voluntary charity meet the case so well; and since all are liable to these terrible calamities, it is proper that all should aid, under the control of the State, in making suitable provision for unfortunates of this class.

To guard well the public health; to provide for the common defense; to preserve the public peace; to secure to every man the reward of his own toil; to secure freedom to worship according to the dictates of one's own conscience, and to distribute equally the public burdens, are among the proper functions of the State. Let Michigan be tried by any or all of these, and she will not be found wanting. Her brief career of less than two score years, has marked a progress in all those things that characterize a well developed State, that gives her a high position amongst her sister States of the Union. She is to-day, the "New England of the Northwest" in many of those things which should characterize a free State. Time will not permit me to present the details of what has been achieved under these several heads, but the steady and rapid progress in our educational institutions, challenges attention, even in this hasty sketch. Thirty years ago, Detroit, Michigan's chief city, had a population of a little more than 10,000. She had not at that time a public or common school, as they were called, of any kind,—much less a "free school," in the whole city. And now the number of children enrolled in schools absolutely free, is greater by at least three thousand, than the whole population at that time; and that city appropriates for the maintenance of her free schools this year, $161,150.00. These schools had worked so efficiently, that on the first of June, 1870, notwithstanding the rapid growth and large influx of foreign population, it was found, by the census, that the whole number of persons above the age of ten years, who could not read, was only about six and eight-tenths per cent of the entire population, and of them five and five-tenths per cent were foreign born, and only one and three-tenths native born. On the 1st of June, 1870, less than four-sevenths of the population of Detroit were native born, but only about one-sixth of the children in attendance were of foreign birth; showing that if our citizens of foreign birth had availed themselves of the advantage of the schools, to the same extent as did those to the manor born, the illiteracy of the city would have been reduced to still smaller proportions. But the tax-payers of our commercial metropolis should count themselves more than paid, by results so encouraging.

Results have been equally satisfactory throughout the State. By the returns of 1872 it appears we had 79 stone school-houses, 595 brick, 4,153 frame, and 591 constructed of logs,—in all 5,418, and they were of the aggregate value of $7,470,-339.00. Their value had nearly quadrupled in the eight years immediately preceding, and public opinion is growing stronger and more healthy every day. The number of graded schools was 292. The whole number attending school that year was 303,212. The whole number of qualified teachers was 11,642, and the whole amount paid for teachers' wages was $1,658,-891.54. The various denominational schools have, in their limited sphere, contributed to the education of the people. The State Normal School and our various colleges have helped to swell the army of qualified teachers. The University is the pride of the State,—an honor to the Nation,—and is destined

5

to share the glories of the world of letters, with the older institutions of the world.

The beneficial effects of these various educational institutions are apparent in the character of our population for general intelligence, morality, and patriotism. The census returns give rank to Michigan on the score of literacy, of which she may well be proud. The whole number of persons in the State, above the age of ten years, who could not read, was, on the first of June, 1870, 34,613; or less than three per cent of our population. The whole number of persons, at that time, in Massachusetts, above the age of ten years, unable to read, was 74,935, or more than five per cent of her population. In like manner, the census shows we beat Connecticut, Vermont, and Rhode Island,—all the New England States, except two,—Maine and New Hampshire. Outside of New England and east of the Rocky Mountains we excel every State except Iowa. Something may be conceded to inaccuracies in collecting statistics, and the varying force of obstacles to be overcome in diffferent States, such as rapid growth of large cities, and the influx of different elements of foreign immigration. It is probably owing to causes like these, that Maine and New Hampshire make a better showing than Massachusetts and Connecticut,—and that Iowa beats Michigan. But after making due allowance, the results show with sufficient accuracy the power and value of the institutions themselves, and the fidelity of administration. Other States have done, and are doing, well, in building up and sustaining educational institutions; particularly the Northwestern States, (some of which we are glad to see represented here to-day). It is in no spirit of boasting that we have made these comparisons, but that we may do justice to the foresight, the wisdom, and the patriotism of the early founders of our comparatively new State, and the fidelity and vigor of all succeeding administrations.

I trust I may be pardoned for lingering a little on this,—to me, a most interesting theme. Those of us who have passed the meridian of life, and whose heads are already whitening for the grave, naturally look to the inheritance that is to descend to our children, as the chief earthly good. And since intelligence and virtue are the only true basis of free government, we know that this inheritance may prove a blessing or a curse, according to the knowledge, the culture, and the character of future citizens. It has been well said, that "culture should be placed above knowledge, and character should be placed above culture." It is not to be expected that new States, while comparatively poor, and wringing their bread from the sweat of their faces, should furnish so many scholars of a high grade, as the older and wealthy States. But it is essential that they should disseminate the knowledge they do have, through all their borders, to every hamlet and cottage in the land.

Michigan has had sixteen Governors and acting Governors; and following the lead of the first, every one of them has proved faithful and true to these sacred trusts. To us it is a matter of joy as well as of pride and exultation, that amidst all the political strife and turmoil that characterize a new State of a somewhat heterogeneous population, amidst all the "ups and downs," the "outs and ins" of political warfare,—no party or faction in this State has disgraced itself by putting sacreligious hands upon our "trust funds." All honor, then, to the memory of Stevens T. Mason, and honor to all his successors,—living or dead; for whatever we may think of their political creeds or minor faults, they proved true and faithful to these essential interests of the State. To you, sir, and to the present Legislature, we look with hope and with entire confidence, that your administration will prove no exception, in this respect, to those that have gone before. We invoke you, one and all, by all those ties that bind good men to their country; we entreat you, as you would not "plant thorns in your dying pillows," that you foster institutions for the unfortunate,—the deaf, the dumb, the blind, the insane, and that you stand "four square" against every attack, *open* or *covert,* upon our educational and other trust funds!

FELLOW-CITIZENS—Thirty-seven years ago our fathers modestly pointed to this peninsula, as a place well fitted to become the seat of a prosperous and free State. Since that time its exceeding fertility has been demonstrated. It has been made to yield, in great abundance and variety, food for the service of man and beast; it has poured forth mineral treasures that have astonished the world; its forests have yielded their wealth in rich profusion; it has gathered a large population of industrious, moral, and happy citizens. These people are well organized into a body politic; they have enacted equal and just laws; they have a judiciary unimpeached and unimpeachable; they have faithfully executed their own laws; they have established and maintained asylums for the unfortunate of every class; they have built school-houses of every grade,—from the little frame that shivers in the wind, at the cross-roads, up to the noble structures of the graded schools that adorn all our villages; and on through our colleges, to the University,—which is at once, an honor to the State and Nation. They have made the means of education to every child, as free as the water that runs or the air that is breathed. By sending more than ninety thousand soldiers to defend the life of the Nation, they have demonstrated their ability to defend themslves in any emergency; in short, having established and maintained all those institutions, and performed all those acts that should characterize a great and free State, may we not, without presumption now say: If you seek a beautiful peninsula, look! And if you seek a great, prosperous and free State, here it is!

For such a State we build a new Capitol. We this day lay its corner-stone. It will be the third, in the order of time, occupied by the State; the first in the fitness of its appointment. Our first Capitol was inherited from the general government. It came as a sort of "dower," when we laid aside our territorial swaddling clothes. In it was written the first ten years of our State history. In it were enacted some wild and extravagant laws, ill-timed and injurious; but in it were laid, broad and deep, the foundations of the State, which will remain after we and our errors have been forgotten. On the whole, its ten years' history was an honorable one. Its location was deemed unsatisfactory, and it gave place to a very modest successor, that sprung up upon a school section in an unbroken wilderness. Venerable old structure! It was not to be outdone in the great cause of education. While its successor was privileged to augment the school fund, by changing a school section from a wilderness to a prosperous city, it forthwith became the pioneer of all our graded schools. It still holds its place,—though dead, it yet speaks. It is dead as "The Capitol," but it stands a monument of usefulness. Like Samson of old, it slew more enemies of the State, by its death, than during all its life. Venerable old building! first useful as a court-house, then as a territorial and State Capitol, but sublime as the model school-house; long may your dome beckon our generous youth to your portals! long may your spire point to heaven!

Our present State Capitol was built at a cost of $22,513 02. It used to be said in derision, that Gov. Barry paid for it by cutting and selling the hay in the old Capitol yard. That he did sell the hay, and carefully put the money in the treasury, is true; an act trifling in itself, but when taken as an index of the rigid economy and stern integrity that characterized all his acts, it does him great honor. It was a time of great financial embarrassment, and John S. Barry has left a reputation for the practice of these sterling virtues that no ridicule can injure. Trifling as was the cost of the rude structure, in it twenty-seven years of our history has been written; in it have been developed and recognized principles; around it cluster associations of more value than marble walls or gilded spires; in it have been recognized the rights of man as man; in it our infant State has grown to manhood. Its successor is to cost more than fifty times as much money. But, although fifty fold more in cost, such has been the improvement in our financial condition that we can pay for this one easier now, than we did the other twenty-seven years ago. Our State debt was as large then as now. The current annual interest and expenses had then, as now, to be met mainly by taxation. But the taxable basis is now twenty-five fold greater than then, and such rate per cent as was necessary then to barely meet imperative demands for interest and expenses, would, if levied upon our present enlarged basis, produce a surplus that would pay the cost of this imposing structure, long before the echoes of the mechanic's hammer can die away. Let then the new Capitol arise in its splendor and magnificence, and let it stand as an emblem of our advanced position; of the abounding prosperity of the State and of our people. Twenty-seven years ago the hardy pioneers were pushing their way into Michigan's forests. The first work was to cut logs for the rude cabin. The neighbors helped to place the logs in position. A little lumber, a little glass, and a few nails demanded a score of dollars in money. There was the rub! But they struggled on,—they triumphed! For their State they built a Capitol at a cost of $22,513 02, and had a hard struggle to pay for it. But economy and labor conquered. The forests receded before their brawny arms; their waving harvests yielded up their wealth; the rude cabins have long since given place to neatly-painted farm-houses, built and paid for with far less sacrifice than their rude predecessors. And now these same pioneers are gathered here with upturned faces,—"with looks intent" and glistening eyes, to lay broad and deep, the foundations of a Capitol, worthy of their State, worthy of themselves. Here let it rise, and let it stand as a symbol of the citizens' triumphs, and of the State's progress. And let the old one stand, until the destroying tooth of time has done its utmost, as a monument of the integrity and struggles of the times that produced it. Then shall our children and our children's children, as they look on this and on that, "thank God and take courage," and move on to the more perfect development of a system of government, that shall recognize in their rights, every citizen as a citizen, and no citizen as anything more than a citizen,—and every man as a man, and no man anything more than a man.

And let all the people say Amen and Amen.

MASONIC CEREMONIES.

Hugh McCurdy, Grand Master of the Grand Lodge of Michigan, being in his place, was addressed by the Governor, as follows:

Sir—It seems most fitting that your ancient and honorable fraternity should be invited to perform the ceremony of laying the corner-stone of the new Capitol of the State of Michigan, and I now invite you to do this, with the usual forms of Masonry.

The Grand Master then responded as follows:

By invitation of the Governor of Michigan, and of the committee in charge, I am here in behalf the Fraternity of Ancient, Free and Accepted Masons of the State of Michigan, and on the part of the Grand Lodge of the State, to perform, with them, the interesting ceremony of laying this corner-stone. Free Masons were originally a company of builders, whose monuments of matchless skill now adorn the world and challenge the admiration of the earth,—masterly models for modern imitation,—which had existed ever since symmetry began and harmony displayed her charms. They were associated not only for the promotion of architectural science, but for the maintenance of that high order of integrity, which is the dictate of divine law. And, although the hand of time has brought our operative labors to a close, yet there is a peculiar fitness in calling upon the Ancient Fraternity to shape and lay the corner-stone of this contemplated structure, to be erected at the bidding of a young but generous commonwealth, and which shall rival in magnitude and grandeur, many an Eastern temple, that told its silent story to whispering winds, four thousand years ago. Though empires of the old world have risen, flourished, and fallen; dynasties have come and gone, and ages upon ages have rolled away,—yet this fraternity, true to its history and work, and stronger and higher than ever, stands here in the meridian splendor of the nineteenth century, to perform its grand and solemn ceremony, taught by the fraternity that dates its dawn early enough to have had the wise King of Israel for a building master. It may have outlived the circumstances of its origin, and the necessities which called it into existence may have long since passed away, no longer to constitute a distinctive feature of the fraternity; but the hand of time has not been laid upon its grand living principle of charity, which stands to-day, and will forever remain the crowned queen among the virtues, until time shall cease. It may have no more monuments of stone to rear, yet never since the days of Hiram, King of Tyre, did it have a nobler mission than it this day performs.

Springing from the science of light, its shining rays illuminate the world, and shed an effulgent brilliance from every ceremony. Its principles having the sanction of the Great Jehovah, and laying their foundation deep in the truths of His revealed word, still inspire its work to-day. Moses dedicated the Tabernacle in the wilderness, and Solomon the Temple at Jerusalem. Our ancient brethren of Israel, also, dedicated their cities, and walls, and gates, and monuments, and buildings.

The inspired Prophet sang never so sweetly as when he

chanted, " Behold I lay in Zion, a tried stone,—a precious corner-stone, a sure foundation." To commence the building, therefore, on a "sure foundation,"—a tried stone,—a precious corner-stone,—is an injunction from the Great Master of the Universe, and has more to commend it to our observance than the mere antiquity of the custom. In no view, then, is the application of the plumb, level, and square to the chosen corner-stone, an idle ceremony. It must be a perfect square strong and durable, well-formed, true and trusty,—and in these requirements, as well as in the implements we use, every Mason and citizen may see the symbols of that noble manhood, which stands on the plane of equality, and regulates its conduct by the Plumb Line of Rectitude, the Square of Virtue, and the Trowel of Brotherly Love.

On the corner-stone, when it is well and truly laid, are poured the significant elements of corn, wine, and oil,—the emblems of Plenty, Refreshment, and Consolation.

May the blessings, symbolized by these elements, descend upon all who are engaged in the work of erecting this building, to be set apart for the use of the Executive, Legislative, and Judicial Departments of this State; and may the work prosper to a speedy and happy completion, and remain for centuries, a monument to the zeal, intelligence, and liberality of a great commonwealth, and to its devotion to the rights of men, and the honor of God. We are taught as we cross the Masonic threshold, or before we engage in any great and important undertaking, to invoke the aid and blessing of Deity. Our Right Worshipful Grand Chaplain will, therefore, approach the Throne of Grace, and ask the blessing of the Almighty God upon this great work.

Grand Chaplain, ETHAN RAY CLARKE, of New Haven, Macomb county, then offered the following

PRAYER.

O, Thou eternal Jehovah, Grand Architect of the universe, grant Thy blessing upon this State, in all its diversity of interests. Endear to the hearts of this people this Capitol, from the laying of this corner-stone to its completion, and ever afterwards. May that wisdom that covered the top of Mount Sinai, when Thou gavest the law to Thy servant Moses, the leader of ancient Israel, rest upon this Capitol. May this State continue to be, as it has been in the past, a prominent star in the nation's field of blue, even until the end of time, when Gabriel shall blow his trump, and swear that time shall be no longer. Grant this our prayer, for Thy great name's sake. AMEN.

The Grand Master then said:

"Brethren, in accordance with ancient Masonic usage, we will now lay the corner-stone of this great fabric."

The corner-stone was then elevated, and let down to its place, by three motions,—each of which was saluted by artillery and the public grand honors.

The Grand Master said:

"If the Building Commissioners have prepared any articles to be deposited in this stone, they will now present them and a list thereof."

Upon which, the Secretary of the State Building Commissioners presented to the Grand Master, a massive copper box, inclosing a glass casket, hermetically sealed, containing historical documents and memorials, with a list of the same.

By direction of the Grand Master, the Grand Treasurer, aided by the Grand Stewards, received the box and placed it in the corner-stone.

The Grand Secretary then read a list of the contents of the box, placed in the corner-stone, as follows:

1. History of Michigan, enrolled upon parchment.
2. Declaration of Independence, enrolled upon parchment.
3. Ordinance of Congress admitting Michigan into the Union, enrolled upon parchment.
4. Pamphlet containing the Constitution of the United States and the Constitution of the State of Michigan.
5. Copy of Act providing for the erection of the Capitol.
6. Copy of instructions to architects submitting designs for the Capitol.
7. Copy of specifications for erection of Capitol.
8. Annual Reports of the State Building Commissioners, for the years 1871, 1872, and 1873.
9. Copy of Estimate and Voucher No. 13, for September, 1873, showing cost of construction of Capitol to date.
10. Copy of sheet of ledger balances for September 24, 1873, showing payments of each class, for construction, to date.
11. Copies of all blanks used in the office of the State Building Commissioners.
12. Copy of Joint Resolution providing for laying the corner-stone.
13. Copy of invitation to corner-stone ceremonies.
14. Package containing deposits in corner-stone of the Territorial Capitol, erected in Detroit in 1823.
15. The Holy Bible.

16. Reports of all State Officers and Boards for the year 1872.
17. The Legislative Manual for 1857, 1867, 1871, and 1873.
18. Statistics of Michigan, compiled from the ninth census of the United States.
19. Report of Michigan Commissioner of Insurance for 1873.
20. Vital Statistics of Michigan for the year 1870.
21. Michigan School Laws, 1873.
22. Michigan State Gazeteer, 1873.
23. Transactions of the Grand Lodge of F. & A. M. of Michigan for 1873.
24 Transactions of Michigan State Medical Society for 1873.
25. Silver plate upon which are inscribed the names of the Mayor and Aldermen of the City of Lansing for 1873.
26. Lansing City Directory.
27. Catalogue and Manual of the Lansing Library and Literary Association.
28. Copies of all the daily newspapers published in the State,—issue of September 27, 1873.
29. Copies of the Lansing weekly newspapers.
30. Pen used in signing the first Constitution of the State of Michigan in 1835.
31. Impression from the Great Seal of the State of Michigan.
32. Lithographic view of the new Capitol.
33. Gold, silver, nickel, and copper coins of the United States,—coinage of 1873.
34. Collection of copper cents of fifty-seven different years, from 1794 to 1857.
35. Copper half-cent,—coinage of 1835, the year in which first State Officers were elected.
36. Set of Compiled Laws of Michigan, 1871.

37. Detroit City Directory, 1873.
38. Report on crime and pauperism in Michigan for 1873.
39. Manual of Michigan Constitutional Convention for 1867.
40. Catalogue of Michigan State Library, 1873.
41. List of Officers of M. W. Grand Lodge of F. & A. Masons of Michigan, officiating on occasion of laying the corner-stone, enrolled upon parchment.
42. Copy of programme of exercises,—corner-stone ceremonies.
43. Copy of introductory address by Gov. John J. Bagley.
44. Copy of prayer by Right Rev. S. A. McCoskry, D. D.—LL. D.
45. Copy of address by Hon. William A. Howard.
46. Copy of Masonic programme.
47. Specimens of United States fractional currency.
48. United States postal card.

The Grand Architect then presented the working tools to the Grand Master, who handed the Square to the Deputy Grand Master, the Level to the Senior Grand Warden, and the Plumb to the Junior Grand Warden.

NOTE.—The coins deposited, include a specimen of each denomination issued from the U. S. Mint in the year 1873, from $20, gold, to one cent, copper.

The silver, nickel, and copper coins were donated by O. A. Jenison, Esq., of Lansing.

The collection of copper cents, from 1794 to 1857, was presented by Hon. John Greusel of Detroit.

The Holy Bible deposited was presented by Messrs. Tunis & Parker of Detroit.

The newspapers were all printed upon bond paper manufactured expressly for the purpose, and presented by the Detroit Paper Company.

The pen used in signing the first State Constitution, in 1835, was presented by Hon. John J. Adam of Tecumseh.

The Grand Master seated the Grand Lodge, and proceeded as follows:

GRAND MASTER—"Brother Deputy Grand Master, what is the proper jewel of your office?"

DEPUTY GRAND MASTER—"The Square."

GRAND MASTER—"What does it teach?"

DEPUTY GRAND MASTER—"To square our actions by the square of virtue, and by it we prove our work."

GRAND MASTER—"Apply your jewel to this Corner-Stone, and make report."

DEPUTY GRAND MASTER—"The Stone is square; the craftsmen have done their duty."

GRAND MASTER—"Brother Senior Grand Warden, what is the jewel of your office?"

SENIOR GRAND WARDEN—"The Level."

GRAND MASTER—"What does it teach?"

SENIOR GRAND WARDEN—"The equality of all men, and by it we prove our work."

GRAND MASTER—"Apply your jewel to this Corner-Stone, and make report."

SENIOR GRAND WARDEN—"The stone is level; the craftsmen have done their duty."

GRAND MASTER—"Brother Junior Grand Warden, what is the jewel of your office?"

JUNIOR GRAND WARDEN—"The Plumb."

GRAND MASTER—"What does it teach?"

JUNIOR GRAND WARDEN—"To walk uprightly before God and man, and by it we prove our work."

GRAND MASTER—"Apply your jewel to this Corner-Stone, and make report."

JUNIOR GRAND WARDEN—"The Stone is plumb; the craftsmen have done their duty."

The Senior and Junior Grand Deacons, bearing the Trowel and Gavel, then approached the Stone.

The Grand Master, preceded by the Grand Marshal, advanced to the Stone, spread mortar upon it, struck it three blows with the mallet, returned to his place, and said: "I, HUGH MCCURDY, Grand Master of Masons of the State of Michigan, declare this Stone to be plumb, level, and square; to be well formed, true, and trusty."

The Grand Stewards then proceeded to the Stone, followed by the Deputy Grand Master, Senior Grand Warden, and Junior Grand Warden, bearing the Corn, Wine, and Oil.

The Deputy Grand Master then scattered the Corn, saying: "May the blessing of the Great Architect of the Universe rest upon the people of this State, and may the Corn of Nourishment abound in our land."

Response by the Craft,—"So mote it be."

The Senior Grand Warden then poured the Wine, saying: "May the Great Architect of the Universe watch over and preserve the workmen upon this building, and bless them and our land with the heavenly Wine of Refreshment and Peace."

Response,—"So mote it be."

The Junior Grand Warden then poured the Oil, saying: "May the Great Architect of the Universe bless our land with union, harmony, and love,—the Oil which maketh men to be of a joyful countenance."

Response,—"So mote it be."

GRAND MASTER'S CLOSING ADDRESS.

Fellow Citizens and Brethren:—In the name of the Grand Lodge of Free and Accepted Masons of Michigan, I now pronounce this corner-store laid to the glory of the great Architect of the Universe, and in exact justice to all men. As ages have looked down upon our fraternity, so may succeeding ages, and our grateful descendants look back upon this ceremony, and this important occasion.

To Free Masons the one is full of meaning, and is typical of the requirements of the good and just, handed down to us by the best of the sons of earth; the other bids the people of Michigan to be of good cheer, and to remember that the magnitude of any event must be determined by its results of good or evil, in its influence upon the well-being and destinies of men.

The past, in the brief history of our State, has written the story of our prosperity, in words too plain to be mistaken. Its outlines have been intombed in the solid rock, and now, as we hand them down to the long future, of which we can only speak with bated breath, other years, rounding into centuries, are before us. Let not the pride of achievement degenerate into vain boasting; but, accepting the past with feelings of devout gratitude, look calmly and heroically to the future, in a trustful resignation to its unknown ills, and a thankful anticipation of its unreached good.

When Bishop Berkeley, nearly a century and a half ago,

turned his eyes towards this fair land, which we now inhabit, and closed a few prophetic lines of poetical prediction,—

"Time's noblest offspring is the last,"

he uttered no exaggerated sentiment, but a prophecy that has already been fulfilled.

The Assyrian, the Persian, the Grecian, and the Roman empires, the first four acts in the world's great drama, were emphatically empires of conquest, and dominion of man over man, but piercing into the darkness of futurity, the Empire which his great mind foretold in America, was the Empire of Freedom, Learning, and the Arts,—the dominion of man over himself and over physical nature, acquired, as well may be claimed, by the love of liberty, the inspirations of genius, and the toils of industry,—not cemented in the blood of human victims,—and founded not in discord, but in harmony,—of which the only spoils are the imperfections of nature, and the victory achieved is the improvement of the condition of all. In short, it is a conquest, in which man, under the operation of mild and wholesome laws, only subdues his fellow man.

Fifty years ago, this State was an unbroken wilderness. Look now on its present picture of power and felicity,—this lovely Peninsular State, with all its happy homes, its hallowed memories, and beneficent institutions—its budding hopes of coming grandeur and untold magnificence. It has been an era of advancement, before which the coming historian will pause, and, seeing nothing over or beyond its margin, nothing of man's pride, will admiringly linger among its monuments and traditions, as his predecessors halted at the gates of Rome, and tarried amid the ruins of Attica and Greece.

With us it has been a period of colonization and growth, in which an empire has been carved out from the wilderness, and a new nation has sprung up,—like Minerva from the brain of Jove,—grander in proportions, more perfect in organization, more just in conception and administration, than the pompous principalities of the Eastern world.

Illuminated by the wisdom of the past and the experience of all time, it has revealed to us that the political economy of the wisest sages, and the intellect and philosophy of the Augustan age, can be surpassed by the achievements of a few brief years, amid the unpolished denizens of a wilderness.

Within that period, Michigan has sprung from territorial dependence to dominion and renown. Where in all the past of Eastern prowess can ingenuity discover the semblance even of its prototype?

Grateful for the prosperity of the past, and proud of the record which Michigan has already made in the strength of her nnmbers,—the achievements of science and the progress of art,—the conquest in political economy, the triumphs of freedom, the expansion of trade, and the diffusion of knowledge,—let us not forget the great principles that underlie it, and has secured them all; but stand firm in its defense, amid the war of opinions, and the tempest of conflicting passions. It is only by remaining true to the State, and standing fast to principle, that we have abundance in the land, peace in our time, and hope of still better things in the future.

On the rugged coast of Scotland there runs out from the Grampian Hills a rocky headland, known in all time as Craig Ellachie. The turf cottages of Clan Grant are in sight of its hoary head, and its earnest, depending peasantry have for their war-cry, "Stand fast, Craig Ellachie." The wild warriors of the hills, serving in the armies of England, are said by the eloquent March, to have carried that cry around the world; and every time it runs along the line, in making the terrible charge, or resisting the more fierce attack, the brave Highlanders assume to themselves the steadfastness of the rock which looks down upon their distant homes. The remembrance of that rugged and storm-beaten craig nerves the heart of the Scottish soldier when shivering in the icy winds of the north, or fainting in the noonday heat of the tropical climes.

Wherever the hour of peril finds him, and his thoughts wander away off to the home of his childhood, the cry comes from that hoary rock, "stand fast."

And so, from the defenders of the truth, in all time, there comes to us in all seasons the clarion cry, "stand fast." The example of their constancy rises up amid all the conflicts of the past, like the rocky headland facing the storm, or holding the beacon on the shore of the treacherous sea. Let us assume the strength of their faith and courage, and taking up the cry that comes to us from far distant ages, give it new life and power by our fidelity, as we pass it along to all in the service of the State,—"stand fast!"

The Romans possessed a shield, said to have descended from Heaven, which so long as it remained at the Capitol, the sceptre of empire could not depart from the nation. We, too, have a shield, spreading its protection over every vulnerable part of the State, coming from the same Divine Bestower, and which, so long as it remains among us, our prosperity and happiness will be maintained inviolate. It is the people's love of liberty! God grant that this love may warm the heart of every citizen, and protect in its might the citadel from invasion, throwing walls of adamant around the ballot,—

> "That mighty weapon, firmer set,
> And better than the bayonet,—
> A weapon that comes down as still
> As snow-flakes fall upon the sod,
> But executes a freeman's will,
> As lightning does the will of God."

R. W. Grand Marshal: you will please make your proclamation.

This proclamation the Grand Marshal made as follows: "In the name of the Most Worshipful Grand Lodge of Free and Accepted Masons of the State of Michigan,

"I proclaim, That the corner-stone of the new Capitol of the State of Michigan has this day been found square, level, and plumb,—true and trusty,—and laid according to our ancient customs, by the Grand Master of Masons."

The Grand Master announced that the Masonic ceremonies would conclude with the Benediction, which was offered by the Grand Chaplain, as follows:

May the blessing of Jehovah, the Eternal, Invisible, and All-wise God, our Creator, abide with this people, now and forevermore,—AMEN.

Upon the conclusion of the Masonic ceremonies, the entire assemblage united in singing the following

HYMN.

TUNE—*Old Hundred.*

> With one consent let all the earth
> To God their cheerful voices raise;
> Glad homage pay with awful mirth,
> And sing before Him songs of praise.

For He's the Lord, supremely good,
His mercy is for ever sure;
His truth, which always firmly stood,
To endless ages shall endure.

Praise God from whom all blessings flow,
Praise Him all creatures here below,
Praise Him above, ye heavenly host,
Praise Father, Son, and Holy Ghost.

The exercises concluded with the following Benediction, by the Rev. NOAH FASSETT:

May the blessing of Him "who hath laid the foundations of the earth, who upholdeth all things by the word of His power," and without whom, "they labor in vain that build," graciously rest upon the Governor of this State, upon all clothed with Legislative or Executive authority, upon the Mayor and Council of this City, upon the Architect to whom is committed the responsible work of erecting this State Capitol, upon our civil, literary, and religious institutions. And may the enlightening, the purifying, and the guiding influences of the Holy Ghost richly rest upon the whole people of this Commonwealth, and the grace of our Lord and Saviour, Jesus Christ, be upon, and abide with you all, evermore,—AMEN.

HISTORY

OF

MICHIGAN

FROM ITS

SETTLEMENT BY THE FRENCH

TO THE

LAYING OF THE CORNER-STONE

OF THE

NEW CAPITOL, OCTOBER 2D, 1873.

TO WHICH IS ADDED

A list of the Principal Officers of the United States, the State Officers and State Boards of Michigan, and the Members of the Legislatures of 1871 and 1873; also, a list of Newspapers and Periodicals published in the State.

COMPILED BY

ALLEN L. BOURS,

SECRETARY OF THE BOARD OF STATE BUILDING COMMISSIONERS.

1873.

Compiled under a resolution of the Committee of Arrangements; the original copy, enrolled upon parchment, was deposited in the Corner-Stone.

PREFACE.

THE preparation of a history, embracing the most important events, changes in government, etc., from the first settlement of Michigan to the present time, is an undertaking involving no small amount of labor and patient research. Among the various histories of the State, published from time to time, few are accurate and reliable; many conflicting statements are found in regard to important events. The compiler of this history has carefully examined all the best authorities now to be found; and especially in the preparation of statistics, has relied only upon official information. Much that is valuable has been gleaned from Bancroft's History of the United States, Sheldon's Early History of Michigan, the Discourses of Lewis Cass and others before the Michigan Historical Society, Lanman's History of Michigan, McMullen's History of Canada, Miles' History of Canada, and Bouchette's British Dominions.

The account of the noble record of Michigan during the rebellion from 1861 to 1865, is condensed from the very able report of Brigadier General John Robertson, Adjutant General of the State. The statements of population are from the official records of the Secretary of State and the United States Census Bureau, and other statistics are obtained from the reports of State officers. The compiler makes no claim to originality in the history here produced; his only aim has been to condense from the writings of others, a concise statement, showing the early condition and rapid advancement to the glorious position now occupied by the Peninsula State.

HISTORY OF MICHIGAN.

MICHIGAN derives its name from the Indian words *"Mitchi Sawgyegan,"* the meaning of which, is the "Great Lake," or "Lake Country," a name peculiarly appropriate from the position it occupies; having Lake Superior for its northern boundary, Lakes Erie, St. Clair, and Huron on the east, and Lake Michigan on the west. The extent of its domain is 56,243 square miles.

Previous to the year 1641, the territory now embraced within the limits of the State, was inhabited only by the red man, though Detroit, as far back as the year 1620, then an Indian village, was the resort of the French missionaries. In 1639, a plan for the establishment of missions in "New France" was formed; but as the French, in consequence of the hostility of the Mohawks, were excluded from the navigation of the waters of Lakes Ontario and Erie, their only avenue to the West was the Ottawa River, through which, in the year 1641, the first bark canoe laden with French Jesuits, was paddled to the Falls of St. Mary, which they reached after a navigation of seventeen days. Charles Raymbault, the first missionary to the tribes of Michigan, returned in the year 1642, to Quebec, in consequence of declining health.

Thus, at this early period, the French advanced their missionary posts beyond the shores of Lake Huron, and to the outlet of Lake Superior.

The first settlement commenced by Europeans within the boundaries of Michigan, was the mission of St. Mary, which was established in the year 1668, by Allouez, Claude Dablon, and James Marquette. In May, 1671, a Congress of French soldiers, and chiefs from fourteen of the Indian tribes of the Northwest, was convened at the Falls of St. Mary, called by Nicholas Perrott, an agent of the French government, at which time and place a cross and a cedar post, bearing upon a shield the French lilies, was raised,—the lands formally taken possession of by M. de Lusson, and the savages were informed that they were under the protection of the French King.

The death of Marquette, on the 18th day of May, 1675, is thus recorded by Bancroft: "In sailing from Chicago to Mackinac, he entered a little river in Michigan; erecting an altar, he said mass, after the rites of the Catholic church; then begging the men who conducted his canoe to leave him alone for half an hour,—

'In the darkling wood,
Amid the cool and silence, he knelt down
And offered to the Mightiest, solemn thanks
And supplications.'

At the end of half an hour they went to seek him and he was no more. The good missionary, discoverer of a world, had fallen asleep on the margin of a stream that bears his name. Near the mouth, the voyagers dug his grave in the sand."

Michilimackinack (now written Mackinac, or Mackinaw),

was one of the oldest forts erected. Its foundation was laid in the year 1671, by Father Marquette, who induced a party of Hurons to make a settlement at that place, as a nucleus for a future colony. At that period, no permanent settlement had been made at Detroit, as the French had a more direct and safer route to the upper lakes, from Montreal to Michilimackinac, through the Ottawas or Grand River. The post of Detroit was regarded alike by the French and English, as a valuable point, and both nations were considering measures for its acquisition. A grand council was called, which convened at Montreal, and was composed of chiefs of the various tribes, from the St. Lawrence to the Mississippi, the Governor-general of Canada, and the most prominent *siegneurs* of the country. This council is described by French historians, as the most numerous and imposing assemblage ever collected around one council fire. In the month of June, 1701, Mons. Antoine de la Motte Cadillac, under a commission from Louis XIV., left Montreal in company with a hundred men and a Jesuit missionary, with all the necessary means for the establishment of a colony, and reached Detroit in the month of July.

"Here, then, commences the history of Detroit, and with it the history of the Peninsula of Michigan. How numerous and diversified are the incidents compressed within the period of its existence! No place in the United States presents such a series of events, interesting in themselves, and permanently affecting, as they occurred, its progress and prosperity. Five times its flag has changed, three different sovereignties have claimed its allegiance, and since it has been held by the United States, its government has been thrice transferred;

twice it has been besieged by the Indians, once captured in war, and once burned to the ground." *

On the 13th of September, 1759, a battle occurred between the French under Gen. Montcalm and the British army under Gen. Wolfe, on the banks of the St. Lawrence, resulting in the defeat of the former, and the capitulation of Quebec on the 18th, to Gen. Murray, who was successor in command to Gen. Wolfe, who fell in the engagement; and on the 8th of September, 1760, the French surrendered to the crown of England, Detroit, Michilimackinac, and all other places within the government of Canada then remaining in the possession of France. This action was ratified by the "Treaty of Paris," February 10th, 1763.

In the year 1772 silver was discovered upon the shore of Lake Huron by a Russian named Norburg.

In 1773 a project was commenced for working the copper mines of Lake Superior, and a company was formed for that purpose, under a charter granted in England.

The struggle for independence under the American Revolution was enacted without the bounds of Michigan. The people of Canada, within which Michigan was then included, were removed from the immediate causes of the war. The result of the Revolution was the recognition of our independence.

"By the 'treaty of peace' made at Versailles in 1783, between Great Britain and the United States, it was claimed that Michigan was within American bounds, but minor questions sprung up between the two governments, producing mutual dissatisfaction; and when President Washington sent

---

* Cass' discourse.

Baron Steuben to Quebec, to make arrangements for the transfer of the Northwestern forts, he was informed by Sir Frederick Haldimand that the surrender of the forts would not take place at that time, and was refused passports to Niagara and Detroit." *

By an ordinance of the Congress of the United States, passed July 13th, 1787, the whole of the territory of the United States lying northwest of the Ohio river, though still occupied by the British, was organized as the "Northwest Territory," of which Gen. Arthur St. Clair was appointed Governor.

The ordinance of 1787 provides that there shall be appointed, from time to time, by Congress, a Governor, a Secretary, and three Judges, who should be residents and freeholders within the territory. It further provides that the territory should be divided into not less than three, nor more than five States, and that "there shall be neither slavery nor involuntary servitude in the said territory, otherwise than in the punishment of crimes."

In pursuance of the treaty of November 19th, 1794, Captain Porter, in the beginning of June, 1796, with a detachment of American troops, took possession of Detroit, entered the fort, which the British had previously evacuated, and flung to the breeze the first American flag that ever floated over the soil of the Peninsula State.

By an act of Congress, approved May 7th, 1800, the territory northwest of the Ohio River, was divided into two separate territories, and "all that part of the territory of the United States, northwest of the Ohio River, which lies to the

---

* Sheldon's Early History of Michigan.

westward of a line beginning at the Ohio, opposite to the mouth of the Kentucky River, and running thence to For Recovery, and thence north until it shall intersect the territorial line between the United States and Canada," was constituted a separate territory, to be called the "Indiana Territory," the seat of government of which was established at Saint Vincennes, Chilicothe being the seat of government of the Northwest Territory. Of this Territory (Indiana), General William Henry Harrison was appointed Governor.

By an act of Congress, approved January 11, 1805, it was provided, "that from and after the thirtieth day of June of that year, all that part of Indiana Territory, which lies north of a line drawn east from the southerly bend, or extreme, of Lake Michigan, until it shall intersect Lake Erie, and east of a line drawn from the said southerly bend, through the middle of said lake to its northern extremity, and thence due north to the northern boundary of the United States, shall constitute a separate Territory, and be called Michigan."

The act further provides that the Territory shall have the same form of government as provided by the ordinance of 1787, that the Governor, Secretary, and Judges shall be appointed by the President of the United States, and that Detroit shall be the seat of government.

On July 1, 1805, General William Hull, the newly appointed Governor, assumed the duties of his office at Detroit. On the 11th of June previous, Detroit had been destroyed by fire. Like most of the frontier settlements, it had been compressed within a very small compass,—the streets scarcely exceeding the breadth of common alleys. Gen. Hull at once turned his attention to the subject, and laid out the town in its pre sent shape, the arrangement of which is attributed to Judge Woodward, one of the pioneers of the Territorial Court.

On the 18th of June, 1812, war was declared by Congress against Great Britain. Previous to, and in anticipation of the declaration of war, General William Hull, Governor of Michigan Territory, was appointed Commander-in-Chief of all the forces of the Northwest.

On the 9th of July, Gen. Hull received orders from the Secretary of War, to proceed with his army and take possession of Malden, (which was the key to that portion of the British provinces), if consistent with the safety of his posts. The garrison was weak, and seemed an easy conquest. Having arranged for the expedition, Gen. Hull crossed the Detroit river on the 19th day of July, and encamped at Sandwich, where the army remained in a state of inactivity for nearly a month, when, intimidated by the hostile manifestations of the Indians, and the report that a large British force would soon arrive at Malden, without having made an attack, he recrossed the river to Detroit, on the 9th of August, where he remained until the 15th, the day of his inglorious surrender. A provisional government was established by the British, at Detroit, and a small force placed in the Fort. On the 10th of September, 1813, the victory of Commodore Perry, in the Battle of Lake Erie, resulted in restoring Michigan to the Union, and on the 29th of the same month Detroit was occupied by a detachment of the army of Gen. Harrison.

On October 9th, 1813, Col. Lewis Cass, who had rendered essential service to the Territory, was appointed Governor of Michigan. Congress, in the year 1823, by an act providing for the establishment of a Legislative Council, invested the

Territory with a more energetic and compact government. The Council was to consist of nine members, to be appointed by the President of the United States, with the consent of the Senate, from eighteen candidates elected by the people of the Territory. They, with the Governor, were invested with the same powers which had been granted by the ordinance of 1787 to the government of the Northwest Territory. By that act the legislative power of the Governor and Judges was taken away, the term of judicial office was limited to four years, and eligibility to office required the same qualifications as the right of suffrage. The first Legislative Council of Michigan convened on the 7th of June, 1824, at Detroit.

In 1831, Gen. Cass having been appointed Secretary of War, he was succeeded by George B. Porter in the government of the Territory. During his administration, Wisconsin, which had before been annexed to Michigan, was erected into a separate Territory.

On the 6th of July, 1834, Governor Porter died, and was succeeded by Stevens T. Mason.

In the spring of 1835, a controversy arose in regard to the boundary line between Michigan and Ohio, and the right to a valuable strip of land, to which both laid claim; the former under the provisions of the Ordinance of 1787, and the latter under a provision in their State Constitution. Each party sent a military force to the frontier,—the one to sustain, and the other to extend jurisdiction over the territory in dispute. A high state of excited public feeling existed, but the most serious inconvenience suffered by either party was the apprehension and temporary imprisonment of a few persons. By an act of Congress, passed June 15th, 1836, the Constitution and State Government of Michigan were accepted, and upon condition of accepting the boundary claimed by Ohio, she was admitted into the Union. These terms were exceedingly unsatisfactory to the people of Michigan, who were impatiently awaiting recognition as a State government, having elected their State officers in the month of October of the previous year. A convention held at Ann Arbor on the 14th and 15th of December, 1836, resolved to accept the condition imposed in the proposition of Congress, at the same time protesting against the right of Congress, under the constitution, to require this preliminary assent as a condition of admission into the Union.

By act of Congress, approved January 26th, 1837, Michigan was declared "to be one of the United States, and admitted into the Union on an equal footing with the original States, in all respects whatever."

By an act of the Legislature, approved March 16th, 1847, the seat of government was removed from Detroit to Lansing.

The Constitution adopted by Michigan in 1835, and under which her existence as a State commenced, continued in force until January first, 1851, at which time the Constitution reported by the Convention of 1850, and ratified by the people, at the general election in that year, went into effect, and continues to the present time, as the Constitution of the State.

The Legislature of 1873, by a Joint Resolution approved April 24th, provided for the appointment by the Governor, of a Commission, to consist of two persons from each Congressional District in the State, in all, eighteen members, for the purpose of revising the Constitution, and reporting to the Legislature, at its next session, "such amendments, or such revision to the Constitution, as in their judgment may be necessary for the best interests of the State and the people."

The Governor appointed the following named persons to constitute the Commission:

1st District—	Ashley Pond,	Detroit.
	Elijah W. Meddaugh,	Detroit.
2d District—	Edwin Willits,	Monroe.
	Sullivan M. Cutcheon,	Ypsilanti.
3d District—	Charles Upson,	Coldwater.
	Isaac M. Crane,	Eaton Rapids.
4th District—	Hezekiah G. Wells,	Kalamazoo.
	Henry H. Riley,	Constantine.
5th District—	Solomon L. Withey,	Grand Rapids.
	Lyman G. Mason,*	Muskegon.
6th District—	Ira D. Crouse,	Hartland.
	Lysander Woodward,	Rochester.
7th District—	John Divine,	Lexington.
	Edwin W. Giddings,	Romeo.
8th District—	David H. Jerome,	Saginaw.
	Herschel H. Hatch,	Bay City.
9th District—	Seth C. Moffatt,	Northport.
	James R. Devereaux,	Marquette.

The Commission convened in the Senate Chamber at the city of Lansing, on Wednesday, August 27th, and organized by the election of Sullivan M. Cutcheon Chairman, and Henry S. Clubb Secretary. At the time of closing this history, it is still in session.

* Resigned, and succeeded by William M. Ferry of Grand Haven.

MICHIGAN DURING THE REBELLION.

On the 12th of April, 1861, the news was received in Michigan, that civil war had been inaugurated, by the rebels, at Charleston, South Carolina, firing upon Fort Sumpter. On the following day a meeting was held in Detroit, at which resolutions were adopted, repudiating the Rebellion, and pledging this community to "stand by the Government to the last." By the following Monday (April 15th), when the surrender of the South Carolina fortress was known throughout the land, and the call of the President of the United States for 75,000 volunteers had been received, the entire State was alive to the emergencies and duties of the hour, and the uprising of her people was universal. Public meetings were held in the principal cities and towns; pledges of assistance to the nation in its hour of peril were made, and volunteering commenced vigorously.

On April 16th, Governor Blair arrived at Detroit and consulted with a number of citizens. The State had been called upon to furnish immediately, to the General Government, one Infantry Regiment, fully armed, clothed, and equipped. During the same day a proclamation was issued by the Governor, calling for ten companies of volunteers. On April 23d the Governor issued a proclamation, convening the Legislature in extra session on May 7th.

On April 24th, the Adjutant-General issued an order, organizing the First Regiment of Infantry, and appointing its field officers. The rendezvous was fixed at Fort Wayne, and the various companies ordered to assemble there immediately. The "Coldwater Battery" was authorized, and rapidly recruited. On the 2d of May the companies of the First Regiment were mustered into service, and three other regiments had been formed. The Legislature convened on the 7th, and within four days authorized a war loan of one million dollars, and empowered the Governor to raise ten regiments.

On May 13th, the First Regiment left for the seat of war, fully armed and equipped; the organization of regiments, authorized by the Legislature, was rapidly pushed forward, and the requisitions for men promptly met. In January, 1862, the Legislature was again convened in extra session, and the following Joint Resolution was adopted:

"WHEREAS, The Government of the United States is engaged in putting down a causeless and wicked rebellion against its authority and sovereignty, inaugurated by ambitious men to obtain political power,—a Government, the safety and perpetuity of which must ever rest upon the loyalty of its citizens, and an adherence to the Constitution;

"AND WHEREAS, The welfare of mankind, and the usefulness and power of the nation, are involved in the events and issues of the present conflict; therefore, be it

"*Resolved*, That Michigan, loyal to herself and to the Federal Government, re-affirms her undying hostility to traitors, her abiding love for freedom, and her confidence in the wisdom and patriotism of the National Administration.

"*Resolved*, That the people of Michigan deem it the imperative duty of the Government to speedily put down all insurrection against its authority and sovereignty, by the use of every Constitutional means, and by the employment of every energy it possesses; that Michigan stands firm in her determination to sustain, by men and treasure, the Constitution and the Union, and claims that the burden of loyal men should be lightened as far as possible, by confiscating, to the largest extent, the property of all insurrectionists; and that as between the institution of slavery and the maintenance of the Federal Government, Michigan does not hesitate to say, that in such emergency, slavery should be swept from the land, and our country maintained."

How truly the sentiment of the people of Michigan was set forth by their representatives in the State Legislature, the future success in furnishing men and money for the defense of the nation's honor, will abundantly testify.

From April, 1861, to April, 1865, the entire period of the war, the number of men enlisted and drafted, exclusive of men who enlisted in regiments of other States, as shown by records of the Quartermaster General, was . . 92,729

Deducting from this aggregate the number of men commuting 1,982

Shows the number actually furnished and credited to the State 90,747

When it is remembered that the entire population of Michigan in 1864 was 803,745, and that 90,747 able-bodied men took up arms in defense of the Union, the State may well be proud of the record. No other State in the Union has given to the defense of the nation a more patriotic, intelligent, and moral body of men than those who composed the Michigan regiments; not taken from the worthless and idle of large cities, but mostly from the good and industrious vocations of life.

The payments during the war by the Quartermaster-General, for bounties, premiums for recruits, and other war purposes, amount to $2,784,408.00; the payments by counties, cities, and townships for same purposes, amount to $10,173,336.79; the payments by counties for relief of soldiers' families amount to $3,591,248.12; making an aggregate of $16,548,992.91, besides liberal appropriations by the State for the relief of disabled and destitute soldiers.

CASUALTIES OF THE WAR.

The State of Michigan, gratefully realizing and duly appreciating the noble sacrifice of life made by so many of her gallant sons upon the altar of their country's liberty, who fell while bravely contending for our national life, and honoring the State; desiring to perpetuate their memory by inscribing their names upon a roll of imperishable honor, to pass into the future as a bright and lasting record of their patriotism and true devotion to American nationality and freedom, worthy the highest and purest veneration of their fellow-countrymen for all coming time; through her Legislature, by a Joint Resolution, approved April 3d, 1869, caused the compilation upon parchment, under the direction of Gen. John Robertson, Adjutant General, of a "Roll of Honor" of Michigan soldiers who fell in battle, or who died of wounds or of disease. This roll is deposited in the State Library, and contains the names of 357 commissioned officers, and 14,466 enlisted men,—a total of 14,823 men,—who fell in defense of their nation's honor, from the year 1861 to 1865.

INSTITUTIONS OF THE STATE.

EDUCATIONAL.

The ordinance of Congress, passed in 1787, providing "for the government of the Territory of the United States, northwest of the river Ohio," declared that "religion, morality, and knowledge, being necessary to good government and the happiness of mankind, schools and the means of education shall forever be encouraged."

PRIMARY SCHOOLS.

By the terms of an ordinance of Congress, adopted in 1785, in regard to the disposal of lands in the western territory, it was provided that section numbered sixteen of every township should be reserved for the maintenance of public schools within such township.

The Legislative Council of the Territory, in 1827, provided for the establishment of public schools in every township containing fifty inhabitants or householders. The first Constitution of the State, adopted in 1835, declares in its article "Education:"

"The Legislature shall encourage, by all suitable means, the promotion of intellectual, scientifical, and agricultural improvement. The proceeds of all lands that have been or hereafter may be granted by the United States to this State, for the support of schools, which shall hereafter be sold or disposed of, shall be and remain a perpetual fund, the interest of which, together with the rents of all such unsold lands shall be inviolably appropriated to the support of schools throughout the State."

The same general provisions are retained in the present Constitution, adopted in 1850.

The whole amount of primary school lands derived from the reserve of the sixteenth section, and sold by the State, to the close of the fiscal year, 1872, as shown by the records of the State Land Office, is 619,864 56-100 acres, leaving 401,751 22-100 acres unsold, with about 50,000 acres yet to be selected and placed at the disposition of the State Land Office, on account of sales which had been made from sections numbered sixteen, previous to the enactment by Congress of the ordinance dedicating these lands to the primary school fund.

During the past ten years the amount of primary school interest, apportioned to the several counties in the month of May in each year, has ranged from forty-five to fifty cents for each child between the ages of five and twenty years. In 1864 the number of children was 272,607, and the amount apportioned at fifty cents for each child $136,362.00. In 1873 the number of children was 400,062, and the amount apportioned was $196,176.80, being forty-nine cents for each child between the ages of five and twenty years.

THE UNIVERSITY.

In the year 1817, when the administration of the territorial government was vested in a Governor and Judges, an act was adopted, providing for the establishment of the University of Michigan.

The first State Legislation in this direction was an act of the Legislature, approved March 18, 1837, entitled "An act to provide for the organization and government of the 'University of Michigan.'" The objects, as set forth in the act, to be "to provide the inhabitants of the State with the means of acquiring a thorough knowledge of the various branches of literature, science and the arts." The act provides for the government of the institution, and for its division in three departments, as follows, viz:

First, The department of literature, science, and the arts;

Second, The department of law;

Third, The department of medicine.

By an act approved March 20, 1837, the University was located in the village of Ann Arbor.

On September 20th, 1842, the collegiate department was first opened, and a preparatory school was also opened for the reception of such as might wish to qualify themselves to enter the University.

The Board of Regents in their report in January, 1847, announced the adoption of measures for the organization of a Medical Department, by constituting three professorships, one each of Anatomy, Materia Medica, and Pharmacy and Medical Jurisprudence. At this time the number of students in the department of literature was 38.

The number of students in the University at the close of the year 1872, is as follows:

Department of Literature, Science, and the Arts, . .	476
Department of Medicine and Surgery, ...	357
Department of Law, ...	331
	1164
Deduct for student counted in two departments . .	1
Total number of students	1163

Connected with the University are a central building, 347 feet in length, for the department of arts and sciences; buildings for the departments of law and medicine, a chemical laboratory, and an astronomical observatory; besides buildings for residences for the president and professors, the cost of all of which was about $230,000.00.

The grounds occupied by the University are 44½ acres in extent.

The officers of the University, on the first of January, 1873, were as follows:

JAMES BURRILL ANGELL, LL. D., . . . President.

BOARD OF REGENTS.

Hon. EDWARD C. WALKER, ... Detroit.
Hon. GEORGE WILLARD, ... Battle Creek.
Hon. THOMAS D. GILBERT, . . . Grand Rapids.
Hon. HIRAM A. BURT, ... Marquette.
Hon. JOSEPH ESTABROOK, ... Ypsilanti.
Hon. JONAS H. McGOWAN, ... Coldwater.
Hon. CLADIUS B. GRANT, ... Ann Arbor.
Hon. CHARLES RYND, ... Adrian.

HENRY D. BENNETT, Esq., . . Secretary and Steward.
Hon. J. M. WHEELER, ... Treasurer.
Hon. DANIEL B. BRIGGS, M. A., Supt. of Public Instruction.

THE NORMAL SCHOOL.

The State Normal School is located at Ypsilanti, was established by an act of the Legislature approved March 28th, 1849, and erected in 1851-2.

The number of students in attendance in the Normal department, in the year 1872, was as follows:

Male, ...	120
Female, ...	176
Total, ...	296

The grounds connected with the institution are five acres in extent. The buildings, two in number, cost thirty thousand dollars.

The School is under the management and direction of the State Board of Education. Rev. JOSEPH ESTABROOK, M. A., Principal.

AGRICULTURAL COLLEGE.

The Agricultural College is located about three miles east from the city of Lansing, in the township of Meridian; was established by an act of the Legislature, approved February 12th, 1855, and was opened for the reception of students in May, 1857. Connected with the College is a farm containing about 676½ acres, and embracing every variety of soil. The number of students in attendance on January 1st, 1873, was as follows: Male, 127; female, 4; total, 131.

The value of the property, as ascertained by an inventory on the 1st of December, 1872, is as follows:

Farm, 676½ acres, ...	$47,320 00
Buildings, ...	116,500 00
Stock, farm implements, furniture, library, etc., .	28,170 40
Total valuation, ...	$191,990 40

The college is under the supervision of the State Board of Agriculture, which is composed of the following persons:

Hon. HEZEKIAH G. WELLS, President, . . Kalamazoo.
Hon. ORAMEL HOSFORD, ... Olivet.
Hon. J. WEBSTER CHILDS, ... Ypsilanti.
Hon. GEORGE W. PHILLIPS, ... Romeo.
FRANKLIN WELLS, Esq., ... Constantine.
A. S. DYCKMAN, Esq., ... South Haven.
Hon. JOHN J. BAGLEY, Governor, *ex officio.*
Hon. T. C. ABBOT, LL. D., President College, *ex officio.*

WILLIAM H. MARSTON, Secretary.

STATE PUBLIC SCHOOL.

The Legislature, in the session of 1869, passed a Joint Resolution providing for the appointment by the Governor, of a Commission, consisting of three persons, to examine into the discipline and general management of the Penal, Reformatory, and Charitable Institutions of the State, and to report plans and recommendations for their improvement. In the examinations by the Commission, it was found that there were contained in the poor-houses, a large number of children of paupers and indigent people, whose condition was most deplorable; and they recommended that some system of State agency should be adopted to receive these children, and provide for their moral and mental improvement, and thereby enable them to fill, in the future, positions of usefulness and respectability. By an act of the Legislature, approved April 17, 1871, Commissioners were provided for, to be appointed by the Governor, to locate the "State Public School," and to construct the necessary buildings. The City of Coldwater proposed to the Commissoners, in consideration of the School being located at that city, a donation of a tract containing twenty-seven acres of land, valued at $5,000.00, and $25,000.00 in money. The proposal was accepted, and a contract entered into to erect a main building, containing school rooms, offices, reception rooms, dining room, laundry, kitchen, etc., besides hospital and rooms for Superintendent; also, seven cottages, each capable of accommodating thirty children. In addition to the land donated by the City of Coldwater, nine acres have been purchased by the State, making in all, a tract of thirty-six acres. The School will be ready for the reception of children, about the first of January, 1874.

The value of the land, and buildings when completed, will be a little over $100,000.00.

The School is under the direction of the following Board of Commissioners:

Hon. JOHN J. BAGLEY, President, *ex officio.*

Hon. CALEB D. RANDALL, Secretary and Treasurer.

Hon. CHARLES E. MICKLEY.

Hon. JULIUS S. BARBER.

CHARITABLE INSTITUTIONS.

ASYLUM FOR THE INSANE.

The Asylum for the Insane is located in the village of Kalamazoo, and was established under an act of the Legislature, approved April 3, 1848. The erection of buildings was commenced in the year 1854, and the whole building completed in 1869.

The erection of the "Asylum Extension" was authorized by the Legislature by an act approved April 12, 1871; the work of building commenced during the same month; the centre and north wing are nearly completed, and the whole building will probably be finished within a few months.

The Asylum was first opened for the reception and treatment of insane patients on August 29, 1859.

The number of patients under treatment on January 1, 1873, was 313, and the whole number since the opening of the Asylum 1,304.

The cost of buildings, land, fixtures, stock, etc., was	$426,846 48
Payments on account of the asylum extension to Jan. 1, 1873	122,614 27
Total cost to Jan. 1, 1873 . . .	$549,460 75

The Asylum is under the direction of the following

BOARD OF TRUSTEES.

Luther H. Trask, ...	Kalamazoo.
Charles T. Mitchell, ...	Hillsdale.
William A. Tomlinson, ...	Kalamazoo.
Joseph Gilman, ...	Paw Paw.
Joseph A. Brown, M. D., ...	Detroit.
Edward S. Lacey, ...	Charlotte.

RESIDENT OFFICERS.

E. H. Van Deusen, M. D., . .	Medical Superintendent.
George C. Palmer, M. D., .	Assistant Superintendent.

J. E. EMERSON, M. D., ... Assistant Physician.
HENRY M. HURD, M. D., ... Assistant Physician.
HENRY MONTAGUE . . . . Steward.
Rev. DANIEL PUTNAM, ... Chaplain.
F. W. CURTENIUS, ... Treasurer.

THE INSTITUTION FOR THE DEAF AND DUMB, AND THE BLIND.

This Institution is situated in the suburbs of the City of Flint, in Genesee County.

The school was opened in the year 1854, in a private dwelling house in Flint.

The building was erected in 1857.

The farm and grounds connected with the Institution contain ninety-four acres of land. The building, and grounds cost about $275,000.00.

On the 1st of January, 1873, there were in the Institution 27 blind pupils and 139 deaf mutes, making a total of 166 pupils.

The management of the Institution on the 1st of July, 1873, was under the following named Board of Trustees:

Hon. CHARLES G. JOHNSON, ... President.
Hon. WILLIAM L. SMITH, . Treasurer and Building Com'r.
Hon. IRVING D. HANSCOM, ... Secretary.

The resident officers are:

EGBERT L. BANGS, A. M., ... Principal.
Mrs. S. C. M. CASE, . . , ... Matron.
Miss M. J. ADAMS, ... Assistant Matron.
DANIEL S. CLARK, M. D., ... Physician.
JAMES B. GIBSON, ... Steward.

PENAL AND REFORMATORY INSTITUTIONS.

THE REFORM SCHOOL.

An act of the Legislature, approved February 10th, 1855, provided for the establishment of a "House of Correction for Juvenile Offenders, at or near Lansing, in the County of Ingham: *Provided,* That a suitable piece of land, of not less than twenty acres, shall be donated for that purpose." A tract comprising about thirty acres was donated by the citizens of Lansing, and one hundred and ninety-five acres adjoining the same were subsequently purchased by the State.

The building was first opened for the reception of inmates on September 2, 1856. By an act of the Legislature, approved February 12, 1859, the name of the institution was changed to the Reform School.

The number of boys in the School on January 1, 1873, was two hundred and seven.

The estimated cost of the buildings is $150,000.00.

The Reform School is under the direction of a "Board of Control," consisting of the following named persons:

Hon. George W. Lee, ... Detroit.
Hon. Eli H. Davis, ... Lansing.
Hon. Daniel L. Crossman, ... Williamston.

OFFICERS.

Rev. Charles Johnson, ... Superintendent.
John N. Foster, ... Assistant Superintendent.

THE STATE PRISON.

The State Prison was established at Jackson, by an act of the Legislature, approved March 3, 1838. The buildings and prison wall cost the State about one hundred and sixty thousand dollars. An equal amount has been appropriated by the Legislatures of 1871 and 1873 for the erection of a new main central building, repairs of wings and wall, and other needed improvements.

The whole number of convicts received since the opening of the prison in 1838, is 4,425, of which number 2,941 have been discharged by expiration of sentence, 550 have been pardoned, one hundred and twenty-four escaped, two hundred died, and twenty-one discharged by reversal of sentence; leaving at the close of the fiscal year 1872, 589 convicts in the prison, of which number six are females.

The grounds of the prison are about thirty acres in extent.

The prison is under the management of a board of inspectors, who hold office by appointment of the Governor; the members of the present board are:

William S. Wilcox, ... Adrian.
Lafayette W. Lovell, ... Kalamazoo.
Albert A. Bliss, ... Jackson.

The officers of the prison are:

John Morris, ... Agent.
Franklin S. Clarke, ... Clerk.

THE SAULT STE. MARIE SHIP CANAL.

The United States, by an act of Congress, approved August 26, 1852, granted to the State of Michigan the right of way, and a donation of seven hundred and fifty thousand acres of the public lands, for the construction of a ship canal around the falls of St. Mary. This proposition of Congress was accepted by the State, and its conditions made obligatory by an act of the Legislature, approved February 5, 1853.

This act provided for the construction of the canal, under the direction of a board of five commissioners and an engineer, to be appointed by the Governor. The work of construction was commenced in the month of June, 1853, and completed on the 18th of June 1855, on which day the first vessel passed through. The canal is one mile in length, having two locks, each three hundred and fifty feet long and seventy feet wide, with a total lift of eighteen and a quarter feet, and cost one million two hundred thousand dollars.

The tolls received for the passage of vessels through the canal, from its opening in 1855 to the close of navigation in the year 1872, amount to $430,542.86.

POPULATION.

The population of Michigan, previous to its final relinquishment by Great Britain, and for a long period thereafter, was inconsiderable, and mostly restricted to the confines of the three principle settlements,—at Sault Ste. Marie, Mackinac, and Detroit. The first enumeration after Michigan became a distinct Territory, was in 1810, five years after the erection of the Territory, at which time the number of inhabitants was 4,762. In the following ten years the population increased to 8,896, and the results of subsequent enumerations are as follows:

YEAR.	POPULATION.
1830	31,639
1834	87,278
1840	212,267
1850	397,654
1854	509,374
1860	749,113
1864	803,745
1870	1,184,282

VALUATION OF TAXABLE PROPERTY.

The Constitution of the State (Article XIX., Sec. 13), requires the Legislature to provide for an equalization by a State Board, in the year 1851, and every fifth year thereafter, of assessments on all taxable property, except that paying specific taxes.

Previous to the year 1851, State taxation was upon the basis of equalization by the Boards of Supervisors of the several counties.

The valuation as equalized for various years, is as follows, viz:

Years.	Valuation.
1838	$42,953,495.61
1840	37,833,024.13
1845	28,922,097.59
1850	29,384,270.66
1851	30,976,270.18
1853	120,362,474.35
1856	137,663,009.00
1861	172,055,808.89
1866	307,965,842.92
1871	630,000,000.00

CAPITOL BUILDINGS.

Previous to the year 1823, when Congress provided for the government of the Territory by a Legislative Council, no very extensive provision was made or required for buildings for the accommodation of the government. In the year 1823 the first State-house was erected at Detroit, for the District Court of the United States and the Legislative Council of Michigan Territory.

The edifice, ninety feet in length by sixty feet in width, and surmounted by a dome one hundred and forty feet high, was constructed of brick, in the Ionic order, having a front portico supported by six columns, the entablature at the sides supported by pilasters.

The corner-stone of this building was laid by the Grand Lodge of Masons of Michigan Territory—Grand Master WHITNEY presiding—on September 22, 1823. In 1870 the board of education of the city of Detroit, in making some alterations to the building,—which had been converted to school purposes,—removed the corner-stone and opened the box, the contents of which were presented to the State during the session of the Legislature of 1871, and are now re-deposited in the corner-stone of the new Capitol.

This building was occupied by the Territorial and State Legislatures, until the removal of the seat of government to Lansing, under an act of the Legislature, approved March 16, 1847.

The frame building situated upon block number 115, city

of Lansing, was ordered to be erected by the Legislature of 1847, by an act approved March 16th, and was first occupied by the Legislature in 1848. The Legislature of 1865 ordered an enlargement of the building, by the addition of sixteen feet upon the south end. The cost of this building, exclusive of repairs, is as follows:

Under act of 1847, ...	$10,503.51
Paid in 1848, ...	8,038.22
Addition in 1865, ...	3,971.29
Total, ...	$22,513.02

In 1853, the Legislature, by an act approved February 14, provided for the erection of "a fire-proof building for the State Offices," upon block number 249, known as Capitol Square, and appropriated $10,000.00 for its construction. The building was erected at a cost of $15,562.00, and soon being found too small for the purpose required, the Legislature of 1863, by an act approved March 14, provided for its enlargement. An addition was consequently made upon the west side, at a cost of $6,482.00, making the cost of the building to that time, $22,044.00.

Governor Henry P. Baldwin, in his message to the Legisture on January 4, 1871, called the attention of that body to the necessity for the erection of a new Capitol.

"The present State House was built nearly twenty-five years ago, when the State was comparatively new, with a population about one-fourth as large as at the present time, and with about one-twelfth of the present taxable valuation.

* * * * * * * * * * *

"The present and growing incapacity of the State buildings, the insecurity from fire of the public records and library,—a calamity likely to result in irreparable losses,—and the requirement of several years' time to complete the building sufficiently for occupation, are, in my judgment, adequate reasons why immediate action should be taken to erect a new State House, with capacity sufficient for the proper accommodation of the Legislature and all of the State departments, and commensurate with the present and prospective wants of the State."

The recommendation of the Governor resulted in the passage of an act which was approved March 31, 1871, providing "for the erection of a new State Capitol and a building for the temporary use of the State offices." The act provides for the appointment by the Governor of three suitable persons, to be known as the "Board of State Building Commissioners," the Governor to be *ex officio* the Chairman of the Board.

It was made the duty of the Board to procure the erection of a building for the temporary use of the State offices, as the fire-proof building, erected in 1853, occupied the centre of the ground designed for the new Capitol, and must therefore be removed. For the Temporary Offices, the sum of thirty thousand dollars was appropriated. A contract for the building was entered into on the fifth day of June, and in the month of November following it was completed and accepted. It was occupied in the following month, and cost, including heating apparatus, $30,693.94. The building was constructed with a view to its adaptation to business purposes, upon the completion of the new Capitol, when it will no longer be required for the use of the State.

In response to an advertisement of the Commissioners, soliciting competitive designs for a new Capitol, twenty sets

12

of drawings were received from architects of various localities, on December 28, 1871. After a careful examination of each, the Board, on the twenty-fourth of January, 1872, adopted the design of ELIJAH E. MYERS, Esq., an architect then residing at Springfield, Illinois, and entered into a contract with him to act as architect and general superintendent of the work until its completion. Mr. MYERS immediately removed his residence to the city of Detroit, and engaged in the preparation of specifications and detail drawings. On the fifteenth of July the Board entered into a contract with Messrs. NEHEMIAH OSBURN & Co., builders, of Rochester, N. Y., and Detroit, Mich., for the construction of the entire building.

At an extra session of the Legislature in March, 1872, the cost of the building, with all expenses incident to its erection, was limited to twelve hundred thousand dollars. The sum agreed upon in the contract, is eleven hundred and forty-four thousand fifty-seven dollars and twenty cents, leaving nearly fifty-six thousand dollars to cover extras, salaries, and other expenses.

The building will be of Palladian style of architecture, which was adopted by the architect, as best suited to the appearance of grandeur, required in a building of this class. The outline is sufficiently broken to produce pleasing contrasts of light and shade; while the architect has studiously observed the suggestions of the Commissioners, in avoiding superfluous ornamentation, preserving solidity and compactness, and at the same time giving to each apartment an abundance of light.

The arrangement of the various offices and departments will be exceedingly convenient; special attention having been given in this respect to the wants of the public, as well as to the offices having business with each other.

The foundation walls to the earth line are of Lamont, Illinois, limestone, in massive blocks, extending the entire width of the wall, and underlaid with concrete to the depth of three feet. The superstructure is to be of sandstone from Amherst, Ohio, and the partition walls and backings to exterior walls will be of hard-burned brick. The girders, beams, joists, roof, and dome, will be made exclusively of iron, of which material all partitions will also be made, except where constructed of masonry. The stairs throughout the building, including steps, risers, hand-rails, balusters, and bearers, will be exclusively of iron. The corridors, from the basement to the top of the building, will be paved with marble and slate. The most approved arrangements will be employed for ventilation, steam heating, and lighting by gas. The basement story will contain an armory connected with the department of the Quartermaster-General, and the remainder of the story will be devoted at present to storage, although the rooms being high, and well lighted and ventilated, will make excellent offices, should they be required at any time for that purpose.

The first story, which will be twenty feet in height, will contain offices and private apartments for the various State officers and bureaus. Upon this floor will be a main corridor, extending across the building from east to west, through the rotunda, under the dome, and crossed at right angles by a corridor three hundred and forty-five feet in length, extending from the north to the south entrance. The rotunda will be paved with hexagon blocks of glass, six inches in diameter, and an inch and a half in thickness, supported by a frame of iron, into which each piece will be closely fitted. From this rotunda, which is forty-four and a half feet in diameter, the interior of the dome, open to the height of one hundred and seventy-five feet, may be seen, with galleries extending in it from each of the stories above. Upon the second floor, at the north end of the building, will be the Hall of Representatives, occupying the height of two stories,—forty feet. This hall will be seventy feet in width, by seventy-seven and a half in length, with galleries upon the east, south, and west sides. The south gallery will extend back twenty-two and a half feet, making the upper portion of the room one hundred feet in length. There will be no columns or other like obstructions in this hall. The ceiling, which is to be of embossed colored plate glass, will be supported by the iron roof-trusses; and the galleries will be supported by iron girders, entirely hidden from view. The hall will be lighted by nine windows on each side, four on the lower floor, and five on the upper, and by a large sky-light in the roof, over the glass ceiling. The gas-light will be reflected down through this ceiling. The Senate Chamber, at the south end of the building, will correspond in all respects but size with the Representative Hall, it being of the same width, but shorter by twelve feet.

Between the legislative halls, at the west front of the central portion of the building, will be the hall for the State Library. This hall will be one hundred feet in length, forty feet wide, and open to the top of the building, a height of fifty feet, with galleries containing alcoves for the convenient arrangement of books.

At the east front, upon the same floor, will be a suite of

rooms for the Governor and his Secretary. Over the Governor's rooms, and upon the third floor, will be the Supreme Court room, with rooms in close proximity for the accommodation of the judges and attorneys, and offices of the Attorney General. The remainder of the second and third stories will be devoted to committee rooms and other apartments required for the Legislature. On either side of the rotunda, a grand stairway rises from the basement to the fourth story; private stairways being provided in other portions of the building as convenience may require. An elevator, to be operated by steam, will be situated in a central portion of the building.

The roof will be made of corrugated galvanized iron, constructed in such a manner that no trouble will be occasioned by the lodgment of snow or ice, and the necessity for repairs cannot occur with frequency. All the windows will be glazed with polished English or Berlin plate glass,—one plate to each sash.

The main pediment of the building, looking east, will contain an allegorical representation of the rise and progress of Michigan, carved in *bas relief.*

The principal dimensions of the building are as follows: Length, not including porticoes, 345 feet 2 inches; depth, 191 feet 5 inches; height of lantern, 265 feet.

The time stipulated for the completion of the building is the 1st day of December, 1877.

CORNER-STONE COMMITTEE.

The Legislature of 1873, by a Joint Resolution, approved April 24, provided for a public celebration upon the occasion of laying the corner-stone of the new Capitol, and for the appointment of a committee to provide for the appropriate arrangements therefor. The committee, by the terms of the resolution, was to consist of the Governor, who should be its chairman; the members of the Board of State Building Commissioners, and ten citizens of the State, to be appointed by the Governor. The committee so appointed consists of the following persons:

JOHN J. BAGLEY, Chairman, ... Detroit.
EBENEZER O. GROSVENOR, Vice President, . . Jonesville.
JAMES SHEARER, ... Bay City.
ALEXANDER CHAPOTON, ... Detroit.
DAVID ANDERSON, ... Bear Lake Mills.
JOHN P. HOYT, ... Vassar.
WILLIAM H. WITHINGTON, ... Jackson.
AUGUSTUS S. GAYLORD, ... Saginaw.
ELLERY I. GARFIELD, ... Detroit.
JOHN HIBBARD, ... Port Huron.
LEONARD H. RANDALL, ... Grand Rapids.
OLIVER L. SPAULDING, ... St. Johns.
WILLIAM H. STONE, ... Adrian.
JOHN S. TOOKER, ... Lansing.

ALLEN L. BOURS, Secretary, Lansing.

THE CORNER-STONE.

The Board of State Building Commissioners was directed by the Legislature to procure a suitable Corner-Stone, and to cause the following inscriptions to be carved thereon, with raised letters in sunk panels, viz.: On the east face "A. D. 1872" (being the year in which work upon the Capitol was commenced), and upon the north face "A. D," and the year in which the building shall be completed. From a number of specimens of granite, from various localities, submitted for their examination, the Commissioners made choice of that from Concord, New Hampshire, as being the most beautiful and appropriate for the use required. A design for the Stone was prepared by E. E. MYERS, Esq., the architect of the Capitol, and a contract for preparing it awarded to Messrs. STRUTHERS & SONS, of Philadelphia.

ANTIQUITY OF THE CUSTOM.

The importance attached to the corner-stone is of very great antiquity. In the Book of Job, believed to be the oldest literary production extant, the Great Architect and Builder of the Universe is thus reported to have addressed the patriarch:

"Where wast thou when I laid the foundations of the earth? Who hath laid the measures thereof, if thou knowest? or who hath stretched the line upon it? Whereupon are the foundations thereof fastened? or who laid the corner-stone thereof?"—Job, c. 38.

The importance of the corner-stone is further acknowledged by the figurative and symbolical use for which it is often employed.

It is recorded in the Book of Isaiah:

"Therefore thus saith the Lord God: Behold I lay in Zion for a foundation, a stone, a tried stone, a precious corner-stone, a sure foundation."

In the 118th Psalm:

"The stone which the builders refused is become the head stone in the corner."

The custom of laying the corner-stone with public demonstrations of great pomp and ceremony, is of very early origin.

The corner-stone of Westminster Abbey was laid on the 24th of June, 1502, by a lodge of Master Masons, at which KING HENRY VII. presided in person as Grand Master, JOHN ISLIP, Abbot of Westminster, and Sir REGINALD BRAY, Knight of the Garter, acting for the occasion as his Wardens.*

In the year 1607, the corner-stone of the Palace of White-hall was laid "by KING JAMES I., in presence of Grand Master JONES, and his Wardens, WILLIAM HERBERT, Earl of Pembroke, and NICHOLAS STONE, Esq., Master Mason of England, who were attended by many brethren, clothed in form, and other eminent persons, who had been invited on the occasion. The ceremony was conducted with great pomp and splendor."*

In 1673 the corner-stone of St. Paul's Cathedral, London, designed by Deputy WREN, was laid in solemn form by King GEORGE I., attended by Grand Master RIVERS, his architects and craftsmen, in presence of the nobility and gentry, the lord mayor and aldermen, the bishops and clergy, etc.*

---

* Preston's Illustrations of Masonry.

The custom of making deposits in corner-stones is of more recent origin, though in very early times coins, medals, and metallic plates, bearing appropriate inscriptions, and profiles of reigning sovereigns and other dignitaries, were placed in the mortar, under the corner-stone; and the stone generally bore an inscription, showing the date and purpose for which the building was erected.

In the corner-stone of the Exchange Building in Edinburgh, which was laid September 13th, 1753, three medals were deposited in "cavities" in the corner-stone, made for the purpose. The stone also bore a Latin inscription on the side upon which it was laid.

The custom now extends to the depositing not only of coins and medals, but of historical records and various memoranda pertaining to the object for which the building is erected, and showing the condition of the country, the State, and the particular locality of the structure, at the time of its erection.

The corner-stone of the original edifice of the National Capitol at Washington, was laid by GEORGE WASHINGTON, President of the United States, on the eighteenth of September, 1793. The building was first occupied by the Government in 1800, during which year the public archives were removed from Philadelphia. The Capitol, together with the National Library, was fired by the British, under General Ross, on the twenty-fourth of August, 1814, and entirely destroyed. On the anniversary of that day, four years later, the corner-stone of the central building of the present Capitol was laid, and the building was completed in the year 1827.

THE STATE SEAL.

The Great Seal of the State of Michigan was presented by the Hon. LEWIS CASS to the Convention which framed the first Constitution for the State, in session at the city of Detroit, on the 2d day of June, 1835, and on the 22d day of the same month, the Convention adopted the following resolution, offered by the Hon. ROSS WILKINS:

"*Resolved,* That the president of this Convention tender to the Hon. LEWIS CASS, the thanks of this Convention, representing the people of Michigan, for the handsome State seal presented by him to the forthcoming State."

The Latin motto on the seal, *Si quæris peninsulam amœnam, circumspice,*—"If you wish to see a beautiful peninsula, look around you,"—was doubtless suggested by the inscription upon a tablet in St. Paul's Cathedral, London, to the memory of Sir CHRISTOPHER WREN, its renowned architect, *Si quæris monumentum amœnam circumspice,*—"If you wish to see a beautiful *monument,* look among you,"—referring to the great master-piece of architecture, by him designed, as the most fitting tribute to his memory.

THE GOVERNORS OF MICHIGAN.

UNDER FRENCH DOMINION, 1622-1763.

Samuel Champlain,	1622-1635.
M. de Montmagny,	1636-1647.
M. de Aillebout,	1648-1650.
M. de Lauson,	1651-1656.
M. de Lauson (son),	1656-1657.
M. de Aillebout,	1657-1658.
M. de Argenson,	1658-1660.
Baron de Avangour,	1661-1663.
M. de Mesey,	1663-1665.
M. de Courcelles,	1665-1672.
Count de Frontenac,	1672-1682.
M. de la Barre,	1682-1685.
M. de Nonville,	1685-1689.
Count de Frontenac,	1689-1698.
M. de Callieres,	1699-1703.
M. de Vaudreuil,	1703-1725.
M. de Beauharnois,	1726-1747.
M. de Galissoniere,	1747-1749.
M. de la Jonquiere,	1749-1752.
M. du Quesne,	1752-1755.
M. de Vaudreuil de Cavagnac,	1755-1763.

UNDER BRITISH DOMINION, 1763-1796.

James Murray,	1763-1767.
Guy Carleton,	1768-1777.
Frederick Haldimand,	1777-1785.

U of M

Henry Hamilton, ...	1785–1786.
Lord Dorchester, ...	1786–1796.

TERRITORIAL GOVERNORS.

NORTHWEST TERRITORY.

Arthur St. Clair, ...	1796–1800.

INDIANA TERRITORY.

William Henry Harrison, ...	1800–1805.

MICHIGAN TERRITORY.

William Hull, ...	1805–1813.
Lewis Cass, ...	1813–1831.
George B. Porter,*	1831–1834.
Stevens T. Mason, *ex officio*, ...	1834–1835.

GOVERNORS OF STATE OF MICHIGAN.

Stevens T. Mason, ...	1835–1840.
William Woodbridge, ...	1840–1841.
J. Wright Gordon (acting), ...	1841–1842.
John S. Barry, ...	1843–1845.
Alpheus Felch, ...	1846–1847.
William L. Greenly (acting), ...	1847–1847.
Epaphroditus Ransom, ...	1848–1849.
John S. Barry, ...	1850–1851.
Robert McClelland, ...	1852–1853.
Andrew Parsons (acting), ...	1853–1854.
Kinsley S. Bingham, ...	1855–1858.
Moses Wisner, ...	1859–1860.
Austin Blair, ...	1861–1864.
Henry H. Crapo, ...	1865–1868.
Henry P. Baldwin, ...	1869–1872.
John J. Bagley, ...	1873

* Died July 6, 1834.

UNITED STATES GOVERNMENT.

MARCH 4TH, 1873.

ULYSSES S. GRANT, of Illinois, . . . President.
HENRY WILSON, of Massachusetts, . . Vice President.

THE CABINET.

HAMILTON FISH, New York, . . . Secretary of State.
WM. A. RICHARDSON, Massachusetts, Sec'y of the Treasury.
WILLIAM W. BELKNAP, Iowa, . . Secretary of War.
GEORGE M. ROBESON, New Jersey, . Secretary of the Navy.
COLUMBUS DELANO, Ohio, . Secretary of the Interior.
JOHN A. J. CRESWELL, Maryland, . Postmaster General.
GEORGE H. WILLIAMS, Oregon, . . Attorney General.

THE SUPREME COURT.

——————————* . . . . . Chief Justice.

ASSOCIATE JUSTICES.

NATHAN CLIFFORD, ... Maine.
NOAH H. SWAYNE, ... Ohio.
SAMUEL F. MILLER, ... Iowa.
DAVID DAVIS, ... Illinois.
STEPHEN J. FIELD, ... California.
WILLIAM STRONG, ... Pennsylvania.
JOSEPH P. BRADLEY, ... New Jersey.
WARD HUNT, ... New York.

* Vacant by the decease of SALMON P. CHASE in 1873. His successor not yet appointed.

SIXTH CIRCUIT COURT OF THE UNITED STATES.

Halmer H. Emmons, Detroit, ... Judge.
Addison Mandell, Detroit, }
Isaac H. Parrish, Grand Rapids, } . . . . Clerks.

UNITED STATES DISTRICT COURTS FOR MICHIGAN.

EASTERN DISTRICT.

John W. Longyear, Detroit, ... Judge.
D. J. Davidson, Detroit, ... Clerk.

WESTERN DISTRICT.

Solomon L. Withey, Grand Rapids, ... Judge.
Isaac H. Parrish, Grand Rapids, ... Clerk.

JUDICIARY OF MICHIGAN.

SUPREME COURT.

Isaac P. Christiancy, Chief Justice, . . . Monroe.
Benjamin F. Graves, ... Battle Creek.
Thomas M. Cooley, ... Ann Arbor.
James V. Campbell, ... Detroit.

THE CIRCUIT COURTS.

1. Daniel L. Pratt, ... Hillsdale.
2. Henry H. Cooledge, ... Niles.
3. Jared Patchin, ... Detroit.

4. Alexander D. Crane, ... Dexter.
5. George Woodruff, ... Marshall.
6. James S. Dewey, ... Pontiac.
7. Josiah Turner, ... Owosso.
8. Louis S. Lovell, ... Ionia.
9. Charles R. Brown, ... Kalamazoo.
10. John Moore, ... Saginaw.
11. Daniel Goodwin, ... Detroit.
12. James O'Grady, ... Houghton.
13. Jonathan G. Ramsdell, ... Traverse City.
14. Augustine H. Giddings, ... Newaygo.
15. Richmond W. Melendy, ... Centreville.
16. Edward W. Harris, ... Port Huron.
17. Birney Hoyt, ... Grand Rapids.
18. Sanford M. Green, ... Bay City.

UNITED STATES CONGRESS.

MICHIGAN SENATORS.

Zachariah Chandler, ... Detroit.
Thomas W. Ferry, ... Grand Haven.

REPRESENTATIVES.

Moses W. Field, 1st District, ... Detroit.
Henry Waldron, 2d District, ... Hillsdale.
George Willard, 3d District, ... Battle Creek.

JULIUS C. BURROWS, 4th District, . . .	Kalamazoo.
WILDER D. FOSTER,* 5th District, . .	Grand Rapids.
JOSIAH W. BEGOLE, 6th District, ...	Flint.
OMAR D. CONGER, 7th District, . . .	Port Huron.
NATHAN B. BRADLEY, 8th District, . .	Bay City.
JAY A. HUBBELL, 9th District, ...	Houghton.

* Deceased Sept. 20, 1873.

MICHIGAN STATE GOVERNMENT.

JANUARY 1, 1873.

John J. Bagley, Governor, ... Detroit.
Henry H. Holt, Lieutenant Governor, . . Muskegon.
Daniel Striker, Secretary of State, . . Hastings.
Gilbert M. Hasty, Deputy.
Victory P. Collier, State Treasurer, . Battle Creek.
Henry D. Bartholomew, Deputy.
William Humphrey, Auditor General, . . . Adrian.
Hubert R. Pratt, Deputy.
Leverett A. Clapp, Com. State Land Office, . Centreville.
Ozro A. Bowen, Deputy.
Daniel B. Briggs, Supt. Public Instruction, . . Romeo.
Cortland B. Stebbins, Deputy.
Byron D. Ball, Attorney General, . . Grand Rapids.
Mrs. Harriet A. Tenney, State Librarian, . . Lansing.
Samuel H. Row, Com. of Insurance, . . . Lansing.
Henry N. Lawrence, Deputy.
Stephen S. Cobb, Railroad Commissioner, . Kalamazoo.
Samuel S. Garrigues, Salt Inspector, . East Saginaw.
M. H. Allardt, Commissioner of Immigration.
Guy H. Carleton, Superintendent of St. Mary's Falls Ship Canal, Sault Ste. Marie.

STATE BOARDS.

STATE BOARD OF EDUCATION.

Daniel E. Brown,* . . . . Saranac.
Witter J. Baxter, ... Jonesville.
Edward Dorsch, ... Monroe.

STATE BOARD OF HEALTH.

Homer O. Hitchcock, M. D., ... Kalamazoo.
Zenas E. Bliss, M. D., ... Grand Rapids.
Robert C. Kedzie, M. D., ... Lansing.
Rev. Charles H. Brigham, ... Ann Arbor.
Henry F. Lyster, M. D., ... Detroit.
Rev. John S. Goodman, ... East Saginaw.
Henry B. Baker, M. D., Secretary, . . . Lansing.

STATE BOARD OF AGRICULTURE.

Hezekiah G. Wells, ... Kalamazoo.
Oramel Hosford, ... Olivet.
J. Webster Childs, ... Ypsilanti.
George W. Phillips, ... Romeo.
Franklin Wells, ... Constantine.
A. S. Dyckman, ... South Haven.
John J. Bagley, Governor, }
T. C. Abbot, Pres't of College, } *Ex officio.*

BOARD OF CONTROL FOR RAILROADS.

D. Bethune Duffield, ... Detroit.
John K. Boies, ... Hudson.

---

* Deceased in 1878.

STEPHEN S. COBB, ... Kalamazoo.
BYRON M. CUTCHEON, ... Manistee.
DARIUS MONROE, ... Bronson.
P. DEAN WARNER, ... Farmington.

BOARD OF COMMISSIONERS FOR THE GENERAL SUPERVISION OF CHARITABLE, PENAL, PAUPER, AND REFORMATORY INSTITUTIONS.

CHARLES I. WALKER, ... Detroit.
WILLIAM B. WILLIAMS, ... Allegan.
HENRY W. LORD, ... Pontiac.
ZEBULON R. BROCKWAY, ... Detroit.
CHARLES M. CROSWELL, Secretary, Adrian.

BOARD OF STATE SWAMP LAND ROAD COMMISSIONERS.

JOSEPH B. HAVILAND, ... Acme.
DAVID J. EVANS, ... Bay City.
SAMUEL H. SELDEN, ... Escanaba.

BOARD OF STATE BUILDING COMMISSIONERS.

GOV. JOHN J. BAGLEY, Chairman, ... Detroit.
EBENEZER O. GROSVENOR, Vice President, . . Jonesville.
JAMES SHEARER, ... Bay City.
ALEXANDER CHAPOTON, ... Detroit.
ALLEN L. BOURS, Secretary, Lansing.

BOARD OF FISH COMMISSIONERS.

GEORGE CLARK, ... Ecorse.
GEORGE H. JEROME, ... Niles.

BOARD OF STATE AUDITORS.

Secretary of State,
State Treasurer,
Commissioner of the State Land Office.

STATE BOARD OF EQUALIZATION.

Lieutenant Governor,
Auditor General,
Secretary of State,
State Treasurer.
Commissioner of the State Land Office.

BOARD OF STATE CANVASSERS.

Secretary of State,
State Treasurer,
Commissioner of the State Land Office.

BOARD FOR EXAMINATION OF CLAIMS GROWING OUT OF SALE OF PUBLIC LANDS.

Commissioner of State Land Office,
State Treasurer,
Attorney General.

BOARD OF CONTROL FOR RECLAMATION OF SWAMP LANDS.

Governor,
Secretary of State,
Auditor General,
State Treasurer,
Attorney General,
Commissioner of State Land Office.

BOARD OF CONTROL OF SAULT STE. MARIE CANAL, AND OF THE PORTAGE LAKE AND LAKE SUPERIOR SHIP CANAL.

Governor,

Auditor General,

State Treasurer.

BOARD OF FUND COMMISSIONERS.

State Treasurer,

Auditor General,

Secretary of State.

BOARD OF GEOLOGICAL SURVEY.

Governor,

Superintendent of Public Instruction,

President of the State Board of Education.

BOARD OF INTERNAL IMPROVEMENT.

State Treasurer,

Secretary of State,

Auditor General.

BOARD TO TAKE CHARGE OF ESCHEATED PROPERTY AND OTHER STATE ASSETS.

Auditor General,

State Treasurer,

Secretary of State.

BOARD FOR THE PURPOSE OF MAKING REPAIRS AND ADDITIONS TO THE STATE PRISON.

Governor,

Inspectors of the State Prison.

BOARD OF COMMISSIONERS TO SELECT SITE AND CONSTRUCT AN ADDITIONAL ASYLUM FOR THE INSANE.

E. H. Van Deusen, ... Kalamazoo.
Amos Rathbun, ... Grand Rapids.
George Hannahs, ... South Haven.

BOARD TO SELECT SITE AND PROCURE PLANS FOR A STATE HOUSE OF CORRECTION.

Three persons, citizens of the State, to be appointed by the Governor.

BOARD OF REGENTS OF THE UNIVERSITY OF MICHIGAN.

James B. Angell, LL. D., President *ex officio.*

Edward C. Walker, ... Detroit.
George Willard, ... , . Battle Creek.
Thomas D. Gilbert, ... Grand Rapids.
Hiram A. Burt, ... Marquette.
Joseph Estabrook, ... Ypsilanti.
Jonas H. McGowan, ... Coldwater.
Claudius B. Grant, ... Ann Arbor.
Charles Rynd, ... Adrian.

BOARD OF CONTROL OF THE STATE PUBLIC SCHOOL.

Gov. John J. Bagley, ... Detroit.
Caleb D. Randall, ... Coldwater.
Charles E. Mickley, ... Adrian.
Julius S. Barber, ... Coldwater.

BOARD OF CONTROL OF THE STATE REFORM SCHOOL.

George W. Lee, ... Detroit.
Daniel L. Crossman, ... Williamston.
Eli H. Davis, ... Lansing.

BOARD OF TRUSTEES FOR THE MICHIGAN ASYLUM FOR THE INSANE.

Luther H. Trask, ... Kalamazoo.
Charles T. Mitchell, ... Hillsdale.
William A. Tomlinson, ... Kalamazoo.
Joseph Gilman, ... Paw Paw.
Joseph A. Brown, M. D., ... Detroit.
Edward S. Lacey, ... Charlotte.

BOARD OF TRUSTEES OF THE MICHIGAN INSTITUTION FOR THE EDUCATION OF THE DEAF AND DUMB, AND THE BLIND.

Charles G. Johnson, ... Monroe.
William L. Smith, ... Flint.
Irving D. Hanscom, ... Romeo.

BOARD OF INSPECTORS OF THE STATE PRISON.

William S. Wilcox, ... Adrian.
Lafayette W. Lovel, ... Kalamazoo.
Albert A. Bliss, ... Jackson.

MILITARY OFFICERS OF THE STATE.

Governor John J. Bagley, Commander-in-Chief.
Gen. John Robertson, . . . Adjutant General.
Gen. William A. Throop, . . Quartermaster General.
Gen. Russell A. Alger, . . Inspector General.

Maj. George H. Hopkins, . Sec'y to Commander-in-Chief.
Maj. John Pulford, ... Judge Advocate.

AIDS TO COMMANDER-IN-CHIEF.

Col. Grover S. Wormer, ... Detroit.
Col. Frank Gorton, ... Sault Ste. Marie.
Col. Robert Burns, ... Kalamazoo.
Col. Charles Y. Osburn, ... Owosso.

STATE MILITARY BOARD.

Jerome Croul, ... Detroit.
Charles E. Grisson, ... St. Johns.

MICHIGAN STATE LEGISLATURE—1871-2.

THE SENATE.

Morgan Bates, President, ... Traverse City.

Lorenzo P. Alexander, ... Buchanan.
Byron D. Ball, ... Grand Rapids.
Homer G. Barber, ... Vermontville.
Josiah W. Begole, ... Flint.
Theodore G. Bennett, ... Jackson.
Robert V. Briggs, ... Wyandotte.
James P. Cawley, ... Morenci.
Isaac M. Cravath,* . . . . Lansing.

* Died May 4, 1872.

JOHN C. DEXTER,	Ionia.
PHILIP H. EMERSON,	Battle Creek.
MYLO L. GAY,	Howell.
GEORGE HANNAHS,	South Haven.
GILBERT HATHEWAY,*	New Baltimore.
BELA W. JENKS,	St. Clair.
EMMANUEL MANN,	Ann Arbor.
SETH C. MOFFATT,	Northport.
EDWARD G. MORTON,	Monroe.
JAMES M. NEASMITH,	Kalamazoo.
LAYMAN B. PRICE,	Lakeville.
ABRAHAM C. PRUTZMAN,	Three Rivers.
UZZIEL PUTNAM, Jr.,	Pokagon.
CALEB D. RANDALL,	Coldwater.
JAMES W. ROMEYN,	Detroit.
ALANSON SHELEY,	Detroit.
FRANCIS B. STOCKBRIDGE,	Saugatuck.
WILLIAM STODDARD,	Litchfield.
WALES F. STORRS,	Coopersville.
JOHN C. WATERBURY,	Lexington.
HARRISON H. WHEELER,	Wenona.
FRANK G. WHITE,	Calumet.
WILLIAM S. WILCOX,	Adrian.
ALFRED B. WOOD,	Saginaw.

HENRY S. SLEEPER, Secretary, Galesburgh.

HENRY SEYMOUR, Sergeant-at-Arms, Grand Rapids.

---

* Died Oct. 26, 1871, and succeeded by SEYMOUR BROWNELL.

HOUSE OF REPRESENTATIVES.

JONATHAN J. WOODMAN, Speaker,	Paw Paw.
JOHN J. ADAM,	Tecumseh.
OSCAR ADAMS,	Flint.
ALLEN C. ADSIT,	Spring Lake.
JOHN L. ANDREWS,	Milford.
MARCUS M. ATWOOD,	Dansville.
HORACE T. BARNABY,	Pompeii.
WILLIAM R. BATES,[a]	Au Gres.
WILLIAM H. BROCKWAY,	Albion.
GEORGE I. BROWN,	Battle Creek.
ALEXANDER CAMERON,	Kalamazoo.
WILLIAM CHAMBERLAIN,	Three Oaks.
HENRY P. CHERRY,	Johnstown.
AARON CHILDS,	Ypsilanti.
JOSHUA CLEMENT,	Jackson.
ANDREW CLIMIE,	Leonidas.
LYMAN COCHRANE,	Detroit.
JAMES M. CONGDON,	Chelsea.
ALEXANDER B. COPLEY,	Decatur.
JOHN F. COULTER,	Niles.
ARCHER H. CRANE,	Blissfield.
GEORGE W. CROFOOT,	Pinckney.
LAWRENCE DALTON,	Dalton's Corners.
PHILO DOTY,	Eagle.
WILLIAM J. EDWARDS,	Niles.
CHARLES B. FENTON,	Mackinac.
RICHARD FERRIS,	Bear Lake Mills.

---

[a] Resigned and succeeded by ISAAC MARSTON.

Asa P. Ferry,	Rockford.
Almon B. Frost,	Oakland.
Samuel M. Garfield,	Grand Rapids.
William D. Garrison,	Vernon.
John Gibson,	Detroit.
George F. Gillam,	Bronson.
Claudius B. Grant,	Ann Arbor.
Robert J. Grant,	Hastings.
Patrick Gorman,	Grafton.
Edgar L. Gray,	Newaygo.
Orson Green,	Geneva.
John Greusel,	Detroit.
Ira R. Grosvenor,	Monroe.
Bernard Haack,	Blumfield.
William Harris,	Rockland.
Alvin N. Hart,	Lansing.
Harvey Haynes,	Coldwater.
John Haynes,	Midland City.
James E. Haywood,	Port Hope.
Ezra Hazen,	Memphis.
Nicholas R. Hill,	Cedar Springs.
Samuel W. Hill,	Eagle River.
Charles E. Holland,	Hancock.
Henry H. Holt,	Muskegon.
Julius Houseman,	Grand Rapids.
William C. Hoyt,	Detroit.
Henry Huff,	Jonesville.
Rossell B. Hughes,	Bellevue.
William H. Hurlbut,	South Haven.
Benjamin W. Huston, Jr.,	Vassar.

SHIVERICK KELLOGG,	Easton.
CORNELIUS KNAPP,	Rome Centre.
JACOB C. LAMB,	Dryden.
JOHN LANDON,*	Parma.
CHARLES D. LITTLE,	Saginaw.
JAMES McGONEGAL,	Detroit.
ELI R. MILLER,	Richland.
NORTON L. MILLER,	Mount Clemens.
RICHARD C. MILLER,	Greenville.
CHARLES R. MILLINGTON,	Constantine.
JOSEPH T. S. MINNE,	St. Clair.
PRESTON MITCHELL,	Marshall.
WILLIAM H. C. MITCHELL,	East Traverse Bay.
MARTIN V. MONTGOMERY,	Eaton Rapids.
JAMES B. MOSHIER,	Linden.
JASON B. NORRIS,	Cambria Mills.
CHARLES Y. OSBURN,	Owosso.
JOHN M. OSBORN,	Hudson.
PERRY D. PEARL,	Belleville.
ORLANDO R. PATTENGILL,	Plymouth.
JOHN I. PHILLIPS,†	Pine Run.
BENJAMIN PIERSON,	Farmington.
SAMUEL POST,	Ypsilanti.
DELIVERANCE S. PRIEST,	Romeo.
ALMOND B. RIFORD,	Benton Harbor.
HORACE D. ROOD,	Lapeer.
ALBERT K. ROOF,	Lyons.
JOHN ROOST,	Holland.

---

* Died March 13th, 1871, and succeeded by HIRAM C. HODGE.
† Died January 8th, 1872, and succeeded by FREDERICK WALKER.

GILES ROSS, ... Highland.
HIRAM D. RUNYAN, ... Disco.
FRANK L. SMITH, ... Jackson.
JOHN J. SUMNER, ... Lambertville.
ALBERT P. SWINEFORD, ... Marquette.
SIMEON M. THAYER, ... Minden.
BRACEY TOBEY, ... Sturgis.
ROWLAND S. VAN SCOY, ... Maple Rapids.
JOHN WALKER, ... Cooper.
JACOB WALTON, ... Adrian.
CHARLES W. WATKINS, ... Wayland.
ALANSON J. WEBSTER, ... Pontiac.
FREDERICK L. WELLS, ... Port Huron.
DARWIN O. WHITE, ... Southfield.
JAMES A. WILLIAMS, ... Quincy.

NELSON B. JONES, Clerk, Lansing.

HENRY UNDERWOOD, Sergeant-at-Arms, Adrian.

MICHIGAN STATE LEGISLATURE—1873-4.

THE SENATE.

HENRY H. HOLT, President, ... Muskegon.
DAVID ANDERSON, ... Bear Lake Mills.
ADAM BEATTIE, ... Ovid.
MARK S. BREWER, ... Pontiac.
IRA H. BUTTERFIELD, ... Lapeer.

J. WEBSTER CHILDS, ... Ypsilanti.
HENRY S. CLUBB, ... Grand Haven.
MOREAU S. CROSBY, ... Grand Rapids.
JAMES L. CURRY, ... Clio.
CHARLES V. DELAND, ... East Saginaw.
GEORGE M. DEWEY, ... Hastings.
RALPH ELY, ... Alma.
PHILIP H. EMERSON, ... Battle Creek.
JAMES M. GOODELL, ... Corunna.
EDGAR L. GRAY, ... Newaygo.
HENRY H. HINDS, ... Stanton.
EDWIN B. ISHAM, ... Negaunee.
NATHAN G. KING, ... Brooklyn.
JOHN N. MELLEN, ... Romeo.
CHARLES E. MICKLEY, ... Adrian.
WILLIAM H. C. MITCHELL, . . . East Traverse Bay.
JONAS H. McGOWAN, ... Coldwater.
JAMES M. NEASMITH, ... Schoolcraft.
ABRAHAM C. PRUTZMAN, ... Three Rivers.
DAVID M. RICHARDSON, ... Detroit.
LEVI SPARKS, ... Buchanan.
WILLIAM STODDARD,* . . . . Litchfield.
JOHN J. SUMNER, ... Lambertville.
WILLIAM C. SUTTON, ... Dearborn.
FREDRICK L. WELLS, ... Port Huron.
WILLIAM B. WESSON, ... Detroit.
HARRISON H. WHEELER, ... Wenona.
MARK D. WILBER, ... Allegan.

JAMES H. STONE, Secretary, Kalamazoo.

WILLIAM P. BURDICK, Sergeant-at-Arms, Saginaw.

* Died 1873.

HOUSE OF REPRESENTATIVES.

Charles M. Croswell, Speaker, ... Adrian.
Francis Ackley, ... St. Charles.
Sullivan Armstrong, ... Newaygo.
Frederick G. Bailey, ... Vernon.
Ira H. Bartholomew, ... Lansing.
Samuel H. Blackman, ... Paw Paw.
Evan J. Bonine, ... Niles.
Thomas H. Bottomley, ... Capac.
Edward Breitung, ... Negaunce.
Edward L. Briggs, ... Grand Rapids.
John C. Brunson, ... Victor.
John L. Buell, ... Menominee.
James Burns, ... Detroit.
Horace H. Cady, ... Mt. Clemens.
James Caplis, ... Detroit.
John Carter, ... Milford.
Merritt N. Chafey, ... Manistee.
William Chamberlain, ... Three Oaks.
Andrew Climie, ... Leonidas.
Thomas S. Cobb, ... Kalamazoo.
Frederick W. Collins, ... Middleville.
Peter Cook, ... Saline.
William H. Curtis, ... Hanley.
Daniel W. Dinturff, ... Fowlerville.
William Drake, ... Amboy.
John F. Drew, ... Jackson.
Henry D. Edwards . . . . Detroit.
Ebenezer S. Eggleston, ... Grand Rapids.
Isaac A. Fancher, ... Mt. Pleasant.

Thomas A. Ferguson,	Sherman.
Conrad Fey,	East Saginaw.
Samuel M. Garfield,	Grand Rapids.
Jan W. Garvelink,	Graafschap.
Arthur D. Gilmore,	Blissfield.
Levi N. Goodrich,	Concord.
Henry Gordon,	Flat Rock.
Claudius B. Grant,	Ann Arbor.
Edward H. Green,	Charlevoix.
John Greusel,	Detroit.
Robert A. Haire,	Spring Lake.
William Harris,	Rockland.
James E. Haywood,	Port Hope.
Christian Hertzler,	Erie.
Alexander Hewitt,	Hillsdale.
Richard M. Hoar,	Houghton.
Orcott V. Hosner,	Frankfort.
Henry Howard,	Port Huron.
John P. Hoyt,	Caro.
Shiverick Kellogg,	Ionia.
George Kipp,	Goodrich.
Alonzo S. Knapp,	South Lyon.
Jacob C. Lamb,	Dryden.
George Lewis,	Bay City.
James K. Lockwood,	Alpena.
Charles D. Luce,	Osseo.
Matthew Markey,	Springwells.
Eli R. Miller,	Richland.
Richard C. Miller,	Greenville.
Preston Mitchell,	Marshall.

CHARLES H. MORSE,	New Haven Centre.
MICHAEL J. NOYES,	Chelsea.
THOMAS O'DELL,	Williamsville.
FAYETTE PARSONS,	Burr Oak.
AARON PERRY,	Oakland.
ONESIMUS O. PIERCE,	Bedford.
DELIVERANCE S. PRIEST,	Romeo.
LAWRENCE T. REMER,	East China.
JOHN T. RICH,	Elba.
THOMAS C. RIPLEY,	Saginaw.
SOLON E. ROBINSON,	Marshall.
ALEXANDER ROBERTSON,	Pokagon.
ELIAS O. ROSE,	Big Rapids.
RODOLPHUS SANDERSON,	Battle Creek.
WINFIELD SCOTT,	Northville.
WILLIAM SESSIONS,	Ionia.
HENRY A. SHAW,	Eaton Rapids
EMERY H. SIMPSON,	Hartford.
LEGRAND J. SMITH,	Addison.
JOHN J. SPEED,	Detroit.
GILBERT STRIKER,	Hastings.
HENRY F. THOMAS,	Allegan.
CHARLES C. THOMPSON,	Whitehall.
GEORGE W. VAN AKEN,	Coldwater.
ROWLAND S. VAN SCOY,	Maple Rapids.
ARNOLD WALKER,	Leslie.
BENJAMIN WALKER,*	Perry.
FREDERICK WALKER,	Mount Morris.
JOHN WALKER,	Cooper.
LEVI WALKER,*	Flint.

* Died 1873.

JACOB WALTON, ... Adrian.
ASA K. WARREN, ... Olivet.
CHARLES W. WATKINS, ... Wayland.
ERWIN C. WATKINS, ... Rockford.
HENRY B. WELCH, ... Monroe.
ERASTUS J. WELKER, ... Kinderhook.
THOMAS J. WEST, ... Milburg.
AMOS R. WHEELER, ... Benona.
WILLIAM H. WITHINGTON, ... Jackson.
DANIEL WIXSON, ... Lexington.
ELISHA ZIMMERMAN, ... Pontiac.

DANIEL L. CROSSMAN, Clerk, Williamston.

EDWARD M. FITCH, Sergeant-at-Arms, Allegan.

NEWSPAPERS AND PERIODICALS

PUBLISHED IN MICHIGAN IN 1873.

ALLEGAN COUNTY.

Allegan Journal, weekly, ... Allegan.
Allegan County Democrat, weekly, ... Allegan.
Lake Shore Commercial, weekly, . . . Saugatuck.
Republic, weekly, ... Plainwell.
News, weekly, ... Wayland.

ALPENA COUNTY.

Alpena County Pioneer, weekly, ... Alpena.
Alpena Argus, weekly, ... Alpena.

ANTRIM COUNTY.

Traverse Bay Progress, weekly, ... Elk Rapids.

BARRY COUNTY.

Republican Banner, weekly, ... Hastings.
Home Journal, weekly, ... Hastings.
Barry County Republican, weekly, . . . Middleville.

BAY COUNTY.

Chronicle and Journal, daily and weekly, . . . Bay City.
Tribune, daily and weekly, ... Bay City.
Zeitung, weekly, ... Bay City.
Wenona Herald, weekly, ... Wenona.
Lumberman's Gazette, monthly, ... Bay City.

BENZIE COUNTY.

Frankfort Weekly Express, ... Frankfort.
Benzie County Journal, weekly, ... Benzonia.

BERRIEN COUNTY.

Niles Republican, weekly, ... Niles.
Niles Democrat, weekly, ... Niles.
Berrien County Record, weekly, ... Buchanan.
St. Joseph Traveler, weekly, ... St. Joseph.
St. Joseph Herald, weekly, ... St. Joseph.
Benton Harbor Palladium, weekly, . . . Benton Harbor.
Michigan Teacher, monthly, ... Niles.

BRANCH COUNTY.

Coldwater Republican, weekly, ... Coldwater.
Coldwater Reporter, weekly, ... Coldwater.
Quincy Times, weekly, ... Quincy.
Union City Register, weekly, ... Union City.
Western Penman, monthly, ... Coldwater.

CALHOUN COUNTY.

Battle Creek Journal, daily and weekly, . Battle Creek.
Michigan Tribune, weekly, ... Battle Creek.
Review and Herald, weekly, ... Battle Creek.
Our Age, weekly, ... Battle Creek.
Marshall Statesman, weekly, ... Marshall.
Marshall Expounder, weekly, ... Marshall.
Albion Mirror, weekly, ... Albion.
Albion Recorder, weekly, ... Albion.
Index, weekly, ... Homer.
Register, weekly, ... Tekonsha.
Health Reformer, monthly, ... Battle Creek.

Youth's Instructor, monthly, ... Battle Creek.
Advent Tidings, monthly, ... Battle Creek.

CASS COUNTY.

Cass County Republican, weekly, ... Dowagiac.
National Democrat, weekly, ... Cassopolis.
The Vigilant, weekly, ... Cassopolis.

CHARLEVOIX COUNTY.

Charlevoix Sentinel, weekly, ... Charlevoix.

CHEBOYGAN COUNTY.

Cheboygan Weekly Independent, . . . Cheboygan.

CLARE COUNTY.

The Register, weekly, ... Farwell.

CLINTON COUNTY.

Clinton County Republican, weekly, . . St. Johns.
Clinton Independent, weekly, ... St. Johns.
Ovid Register, weekly, ... Ovid.

DELTA COUNTY.

Escanaba Tribune, weekly, ... Escanaba.

EATON COUNTY,

Charlotte Republican, weekly, ... Charlotte.
Democratic Leader, weekly, ... Charlotte.
Bellevue Weekly Gazette, ... Bellevue.
Eaton Rapids Journal, weekly, ... Eaton Rapids.
Grand Ledge Independent, weekly, . . . Grand Ledge.
College Express, monthly, ... Olivet.

GENESEE COUNTY.

Flint Globe, weekly, ... Flint.
Wolverine Citizen, weekly, ... Flint.

Genesee Democrat, weekly, ... Flint.
Fenton Gazette, weekly, ... Fentonville.
Fenton Independent, weekly, . . . Fentonville.

GRAND TRAVERSE COUNTY.

Traverse Bay Eagle, weekly, . . . Traverse City.
Grand Traverse Herald, weekly, . . . Traverse City.

GRATIOT COUNTY.

Gratiot County Journal, weekly, ... Ithaca.
St. Louis Herald, weekly, ... St. Louis.

HILLSDALE COUNTY.

Jonesville Independent, weekly, ... Jonesville.
Hillsdale Standard, weekly, ... Hillsdale.
Hillsdale Democrat, weekly, ... Hillsdale.
Hillsdale Business, weekly, ... Hillsdale.
Rough Notes, weekly, ... Reading.

HOUGHTON COUNTY.

Portage Lake Mining Gazette, weekly, . . Houghton.
Northwestern Mining Journal, weekly, . . Hancock.

HURON COUNTY.

Huron County News, weekly, ... Port Austin.

INGHAM COUNTY.

Lansing State Republican, weekly, ... Lansing.
Lansing Journal, weekly, ... Lansing.
Ingham County News, weekly, ... Mason.
Williamston Enterprise, weekly, ... Williamston.
Leslie Herald, weekly, ... Leslie.

IONIA COUNTY.

Ionia Sentinel, weekly, ... Ionia.

Ionia Standard, weekly, ... Ionia.
Advertiser, weekly, ... Portland.
Advertiser, weekly, ... Hubbardston.
Grand River Herald, weekly, ... Muir.

IOSCO COUNTY.

Iosco County Gazette, weekly, . . . Tawas City.

ISABELLA COUNTY.

Isabella County Enterprise, weekly, . . Mt. Pleasant.

JACKSON COUNTY.

Jackson Citizen, daily and weekly, . . . Jackson.
Jackson Patriot, daily and weekly, ... Jackson.
Concord News, weekly, ... Concord.

KALAMAZOO COUNTY.

Kalamazoo Telegraph, daily and weekly, . . Kalamazoo.
Kalamazoo Gazette, weekly, ... Kalamazoo.
Schoolcraft Despatch, weekly, ... Schoolcraft.
Torchlight and Herald, fortnightly, . . Kalamazoo.
Michigan Freemason, monthly, ... Kalamazoo.

KENT COUNTY.

Grand Rapids Eagle, daily and weekly, . Grand Rapids.
Grand Rapids Times, daily and weekly, . . Grand Rapids.
Grand Rapids Democrat, daily and weekly, . Grand Rapids.
Lowell Journal, weekly, ... Lowell.
Wolverine Clipper, weekly, ... Cedar Springs.
Register, weekly, ... Rockford.

LAKE COUNTY.

Lake County Star, weekly, ... Chase.

LAPEER COUNTY.

Weekly Clarion, ... Lapeer.
Democrat, weekly, ... Lapeer.

LEELANAW COUNTY.

Leelanaw Tribune, weekly, ... Northport.

LENAWEE COUNTY.

Adrian Times and Expositor, daily and weekly, . Adrian.
Adrian Press, daily and weekly, ... Adrian.
Adrian Journal, weekly, ... Adrian.
Auzeiger (German), weekly, ... Adrian.
Hudson Post, weekly, ... Hudson.
Hudson Gazette, weekly, ... Hudson.
New Era, weekly, ... Morenci.
Raisin Valley Record, weekly, ... Tecumseh.
Tecumseh Herald, weekly, ... Tecumseh.

LIVINGSTON COUNTY.

Livingston County Republican, weekly, . . Howell.
Livingston Democrat, weekly, ... Howell.
Brighton Citizen, weekly, ... Brighton.

MACOMB COUNTY.

Mt. Clemens Monitor, weekly, ... Mt. Clemens.
Mt. Clemens Press, weekly, ... Mt. Clemens.
Mt. Clemens Reporter, weekly, ... Mt. Clemens.

MANISTEE COUNTY.

Manistee Times, weekly, ... Manistee.
Manistee Standard,* weekly, ... Manistee.

* Two weekly newspapers of this name are published at Manistee,—one by FOWLER, the other by HOFFMAN.

MARQUETTE COUNTY.

Mining Journal, weekly, ... Marquette.

MASON COUNTY.

Mason County Record, weekly, ... Ludington.
Ludington Weekly Appeal, ... Ludington.

MECOSTA COUNTY.

Mecosta County Pioneer, weekly, ... Big Rapids.
The Magnet, weekly, ... Big Rapids.

MENOMINEE COUNTY.

Menominee Herald, weekly, ... Menominee.
Lumberman and Miner, weekly, ... Menominee.

MIDLAND COUNTY.

Midland Independent, weekly, ... Midland City.
Midland Times, weekly, ... Midland City.

MONROE COUNTY.

Monroe Commercial, weekly, ... Monroe.
Monroe Monitor, weekly, ... Monroe.
Dundee Enterprise, weekly, ... Dundee.

MONTCALM COUNTY.

Montcalm Herald, weekly, ... Stanton.
Greenville Independent, weekly, ... Greenville.
Greenville Democrat, weekly, ... Greenville.
Howard Record, weekly, ... Howard City.

MUSKEGON COUNTY.

Muskegon Chronicle, weekly, ... Muskegon.
Muskegon News and Reporter, weekly, . . . Muskegon.
Muskegon Gazette and Bulletin, weekly, . Muskegon.

Whitehall Forum, weekly, ... Whitehall.

Michigan Lumberman, monthly, . . . Muskegon.

NEWAYGO COUNTY.

Newaygo Republican, weekly, ... Newaygo.

OAKLAND COUNTY.

Pontiac Gazette, weekly, ... Pontiac.

Pontiac Bill Poster, weekly, ... Pontiac.

Holly Register, weekly, ... Holly.

Milford Times, weekly, ... Milford.

Rochester Era, weekly, ... Rochester.

OCEANA COUNTY.

Pentwater News, weekly, ... Pentwater.

Oceana Times, weekly, ... Pentwater.

Oceana County Journal, weekly, ... Hart.

ONTONAGON COUNTY.

Lake Superior Miner, weekly, . . . Ontonagon.

OSCEOLA COUNTY.

Osceola Outline, weekly, ... Hersey.

Evart Review, weekly, ... Evart.

Reed City Clarion, weekly, ... Reed City.

OTTAWA COUNTY.

Grand Haven Herald, weekly, ... Grand Haven.

Grand Haven News, weekly, ... Grand Haven.

Independent, weekly, ... Spring Lake.

De Hope (Dutch), weekly, ... Holland.

De Groudwet (Dutch), weekly, ... Holland.

De Hollander (Dutch), weekly, ... Holland.

De Watcher (Dutch), semi-monthly, . . . Holland.

SAGINAW COUNTY.

Saginaw Enterprise, daily and weekly, . . East Saginaw.
Saginaw Courier, daily and weekly, . . East Saginaw.
Saginaw Zeitung (German), weekly, . . East Saginaw.
Saginaw Republican, weekly, ... Saginaw.
Saginawian, weekly,. . . . . Saginaw.
Chesaning Times, weekly, ... Chesaning.

SANILAC COUNTY.

Sanilac Jeffersonian, weekly, ... Lexington.

SHIAWASSEE COUNTY.

Shiawassee American, weekly, ... Corunna.
Owosso Weekly Press, ... Owosso.
Owosso Crusader, weekly, ... Owosso.

ST. CLAIR COUNTY.

Port Huron Times, daily and weekly, . . Port Huron.
Port Huron Commercial, weekly, ... Port Huron.
St. Clair Republican, weekly, ... St. Clair.
Terra Firma, monthly, ... Port Huron.

ST. JOSEPH COUNTY.

Weekly Mercury, ... Constantine.
Sturgis Journal, weekly, ... Sturgis.
Three Rivers Reporter, weekly, ... Three Rivers.
St. Joseph County Democrat, weekly, . . Three Rivers.
St. Joseph County Republican, weekly, . . . Centreville.
Mendonian, weekly, ... Mendon.

TUSCOLA COUNTY.

Tuscola Advertiser, weekly, ... Caro.
Tuscola County Pioneer, weekly, ... Vassar.

VAN BUREN COUNTY.

Paw Paw Courier, weekly, ... Paw Paw.
True Northerner, weekly, ... Paw Paw.
Lawton Tribune, weekly, ... Lawton.
Van Buren Republican, weekly, . . . Decatur.
Hartford Day Spring, weekly, ... Hartford.
Weekly Journal, ... Bangor.
Breedsville Messenger, weekly, . . . Breedsville.
South Haven Sentinel, weekly, . . . South Haven.

WASHTENAW COUNTY.

Ann Arbor Register, weekly, ... Ann Arbor.
Michigan Argus, weekly, ... Ann Arbor.
Peninsula Courier and Family Visitant, weekly, Ann Arbor.
Chelsea Herald, weekly, ... Chelsea.
Dexter Leader, weekly, ... Dexter.
Manchester Enterprise, weekly, ... Manchester.
Saline Review, weekly, ... Saline.
Ypsilanti Commercial, weekly, ... Ypsilanti.
Ypsilanti Sentinal, weekly, ... Ypsilanti.
The Chronicle (University), semi-monthly, . . Ann Arbor.

WAYNE COUNTY.

Detroit Post, daily, tri-weekly, and weekly, . . Detroit.
Detroit Tribune, daily, tri-weekly, and weekly, . . Detroit.
Detroit Free Press, daily, tri-weekly, and weekly, . Detroit.
Daily Union, daily and weekly, ... Detroit.
Daily Evening News, daily and weekly, . . Detroit.
Michigan Journal (German), daily and weekly, . Detroit.
Michigan Volksblatt (German), daily and weekly, . Detroit.
Daily Abend Post (German), daily and weekly, . Detroit.

Commercial Advertiser and Michigan Home Journal, weekly, ... Detroit.
Journal of Commerce, weekly, ... Detroit.
Mechanic and Inventor, weekly, ... Detroit.
Western Home Journal, weekly, ... Detroit.
Michigan Farmer, weekly, ... Detroit.
Mystic Star, monthly, ... Detroit.
Yankee Land, monthly, ... Detroit.
Review of Medicine, monthly, ... Detroit.
Peninsular Journal of Medicine, monthly, . . Detroit.
American Observer, monthly, ... Detroit.
Song Journal, monthly, ... Detroit.
Northville Record, weekly, ... Northville.
Wyandotte Enterprise, weekly, ... Wyandotte.

WEXFORD COUNTY.

Wexford County Pioneer, weekly, ... Sherman.
Clam Lake News, weekly, ... Clam Lake.

COPIES OF DOCUMENTS

DEPOSITED IN THE CORNER-STONE OF THE TERRITORIAL CAPITOL, ERECTED AT DETROIT IN 1823.

HISTORICAL MEMORANDA.

Canada was first taken possession of by the French in 1608.

Detroit became an important military post, garrisoned by the French, in 1683, being one of an extended chain of military posts established by the French in North America.

With other possessions of the French in this part of North America, Detroit was surrendered by that power to the King of Great Britain, by the Treaty of Paris, 1763.

By the Treaty of Peace, September 3d, 1783, it was recognized by the British Government as an integral part of the United States of America.

And in pursuance of the Treaty of the 19th of November, 1794, it was taken possession of by General ANTHONY WAYNE, in the name of the United States of America, July, 1796.

NAMES OF THE OFFICERS WHO PRESIDED WHEN LAYING THE CORNER-STONE OF THE COURT-HOUSE IN THE CITY OF DETROIT, SEPT. 22, A. L. 5823.

GRAND LODGE, TERRITORY OF MICHIGAN.

R. W. Bro. WHITNEY,	Grand Master.
RISDON,	Deputy Grand Master.
SMYTH,	Past Master.
SCHWARZ,	Senior Grand Warden.
H. I. HUNT,	Junior Grand Warden.
J. ABBATT,	Grand Treasurer.
C. S. PAYNE,	Grand Secretary.
C. JACKSON,	Senior Grand Deacon.
J. MOORS,	Junior Grand Deacon.
ROWLAND,	Grand Marshal.
WOODWORTH,	Grand Marshal.
FLETCHER,	Grand Chaplain.
SHERWOOD,	Grand Tiler.

The following coins were contained in the box:

	DATE.
Silver $1.00,	1798.
Silver 50c.	1818.
Silver 25c.	1805.
Silver 10c.	1807.
Copper 1c.	1818.
Copper ½c.	1805.

Also a copy of the "Masonic Mirror and Symbolic Chart," "presented to Monroe Chapter No. 1, by Comp. J. L. WHITING, June 14th, A. L. 5821."

THE END.

www.ingramcontent.com/pod-product-compliance
Lightning Source LLC
LaVergne TN
LVHW021415110826
845150LV00007B/1943

* 9 7 8 1 4 2 5 5 0 9 8 5 9 *